INTERNATIONAL INDIA:
A TURNING POINT IN EDUCATIONAL
EXCHANGE WITH THE U.S.

INTERNATIONAL INDIA: A TURNING POINT IN EDUCATIONAL EXCHANGE WITH THE U.S.

EDITED BY RAJIKA BHANDARI

Third in a series of Global Education Research Reports

New York

IIE publications can be purchased at: www.iiebooks.org

The Institute of International Education
809 United Nations Plaza, New York, New York 10017

© 2010 by the Institute of International Education
All rights reserved. Published 2010
Printed in the United States of America
ISBN-13: 978-0-87206-321-1

Library of Congress Cataloging-in-Publication Data

International India : a turning point in educational exchange with the U.S. / edited by
Rajika Bhandari.
    p. cm. -- (Global education research reports)
    Includes bibliographical references.
    ISBN 978-0-87206-321-1
    1. Educational exchanges--India. 2. Educational exchanges--United States. 3. Education, Higher--
India. 4. Education, Higher--United States. 5. India--Foreign relations--United States. 6. United
States--Foreign relations--India. I. Bhandari, Rajika.
    LB2376.6.I4I57 2010
    370.1160954--dc22
                                        2009053375

Series editors:
Daniel Obst, Director of Membership and Higher Education Services, IIE
Sharon Witherell, Director of Public Affairs, IIE
Shepherd Laughlin, Assistant Editor

Cover image courtesy of Avinash Manekar
Avinash Manekar, "Drama," 2006. Acrylic on canvas. 28 x 36 inches.
Cover and text design: Pat Scully Design

TABLE OF CONTENTS

FIGURES AND TABLES

FOREWORDS

By Allan E. Goodman

India has the distinction of sending more students abroad to the U.S. than any other country, with 103,260 students in 2008/09. But these impressive numbers represent a tiny portion of the many Indians who would like to go abroad for higher education, and only 12 percent of the relevant age group has access to higher education at home.

This figure also stands in stark contrast to the 3,146 Americans who studied abroad in India in 2007/08. This exchange imbalance should compel us to examine our policies and find ways to send more Americans to India. Taking a step in this direction, the U.S. and Indian governments signed a historic new Fulbright agreement in July 2008, effectively doubling the number of Fulbright-Nehru grants for American and Indian students and scholars. Since 1950, more than 5,000 Indian students and scholars have come to the U.S. and more than 3,100 American teachers, scholars, and students have gone to India under the Fulbright banner.

The career of one of the 2009 winners of the Nobel Prize in Chemistry illustrates the benefits of educational exchange. Born in the Indian province of Tamil Nadu, Venkatraman Ramakrishnan studied physics in India and at Ohio University before switching to biology at the University of California, San Diego. He soon began studying the structure and function of ribosomes, which aid in the translation of DNA into living material. These studies have led to the development of new antibiotics, and today Dr. Ramakrishnan continues his work at Cambridge University in the United Kingdom.

This story is echoed in the experiences of many scholars in the Indian diaspora. But in the years to come, I would like to see it play out in reverse, when an American scholar—or better yet an Indo-U.S. team—wins a Nobel Prize for scientific research conducted in India. In order to foster the kinds of bilateral partnerships that may make such exchanges possible, IIE has launched a new Center for International Partnerships in Higher Education. Through a grant from the U.S. Department of Education, IIE will specifically focus on fostering partnerships between U.S. and Indian institutions in the first year of the center's operations.

Through the many scholarship programs we administer, our newly created Center for International Partnerships in Higher Education, and the work of our office in New Delhi, IIE is committed to supporting U.S.-India higher education exchange so that these collaborations can continue to yield benefits for both countries and the world in the coming decades.

Allan E. Goodman
President & CEO, Institute of International Education

BY WILLIAM L. GERTZ

How little we in the United States know about the world's most populous democracy—India.

With its population of 1.2 billion people and an average annual GDP growth rate of 5.8 percent, India is among the world's most dynamic and rapidly growing economies. Bangalore has become one of the world's leading hubs of information technology and is on a par with Silicon Valley or Austin, Texas. Mumbai is rapidly evolving into one of the world's leading financial centers. India's current GDP of $1.2 trillion makes it the twelfth largest economy in the world, and the figure is expected to quadruple by 2020 according to a 2007 Goldman Sachs report.

After a trip to Bangalore to study the information technology and outsourcing sectors, Thomas Friedman decided to write *The World is Flat*, which details the effects of globalization. Friedman asserts that globalization is being spearheaded by the information technology revolution and the lowering of global political and economic barriers, which is leading to a world that is not only more competitive but also more collaborative.

India is showcased in *The World is Flat* as a hotspot of dynamic economic development and one of the 21st century's leading centers of opportunity and human advancement. The nation's rapid development is enabling tens of millions of people to move up the socioeconomic ladder into a growing middle class. The explosive growth of an Indian middle class presents a unique opportunity for those of us concerned with international education.

As India experiences an economic surge, the number of students who will choose to study in the U.S. will naturally increase. India is now the leading country of origin for students studying in the U.S., and the number of students from India has increased by 9 percent over the previous year to 103,260 students, according to *Open Doors*. Indian students are fast learning the value of education in the U.S., especially in the fields of science and technology.

There is also an increasing number of middle school and high school students coming to the U.S.; our own Summer Institute for the Gifted (SIG) program, held on eight U.S. campuses, has recently experienced a marked increase in Indian students.

In the coming decade, we will also see substantial growth in the number of U.S. undergraduates who will study in India. According to *Open Doors*, study abroad in India was up 20 percent in the past year. While we believe this number may fall slightly in 2009, India is clearly on the map as an emerging study abroad destination.

We are pleased to once again partner with the Institute of International Education on our continuing Global Education Research Reports. We hope you will enjoy reading this latest edition and we thank the authors for their fresh viewpoints, innovative ideas, and unique insights.

William L. Gertz
President & CEO, American Institute For Foreign Study (AIFS)
Trustee, AIFS Foundation

INTRODUCTION

PHILIP G. ALTBACH AND AJIT MOTWANI

India and the United States: Converging Higher Education Needs?

PHILIP G. ALTBACH, MONAN UNIVERSITY PROFESSOR AND DIRECTOR OF
THE CENTER FOR INTERNATIONAL HIGHER EDUCATION, BOSTON COLLEGE

The world's second- and third-largest higher education systems have a long history together. In the past two decades, perhaps one million Indian students have been educated in the United States. Many estimates indicate that approximately 80 percent have not returned home. These highly educated Indians have assisted the American economy, particularly in fields like information technology, biotechnology, medicine, and finance. The number of Americans who have studied in India—3,146 in 2007/08—is miniscule by comparison, and this modest number is up 20 percent from the previous year. We can see, from these and other statistics, that the U.S.-Indian higher education relationship is immensely unequal.

Over a half-century or more, Indian students have come in large numbers to the United States to be educated, and the majority have stayed to contribute to the U.S. economy. The relationship has not been entirely in one direction, however. The United States, through a variety of aid and exchange programs, has participated in Indian higher education by assisting in the establishment of agricultural universities, helping to plan and then supporting the Indian Institute of Management and the Indian Institute of Technology, and sponsoring the many programs of the United States Educational Foundation in India. American foundations, such as Ford and Rockefeller, have long been active in India and have occasionally worked in higher education. Still, if one had to create a "balance sheet" of higher education between the two countries, it is quite likely that India has provided more help to the United States than vice versa over the years due to its contributions to America's highly educated labor force.

The relationship has become more complex in the 21st century. What used to be called brain drain is now much more of a "brain exchange" in which there is considerable mobility among countries. A growing number of Indians who are educated abroad return home following their studies. Others, who have settled abroad, create complex relationships with their home countries, setting up companies or investing in India, maintaining ongoing relationships with universities and other institutions, living part time in each country, or making other arrangements.

The Internet and fairly easy international travel facilitate this new binational existence. A number of changes have taken place in India in recent years—most importantly, the unprecedented economic growth that the country has experienced, made possible by opening the economy to investment and loosening the traditionally strict regulations on business of all kinds. Nonresident Indians have recognized new opportunities for collaboration and involvement in many economic and social institutions in India, including in higher education.

Higher Education at the Cusp of Change

India's higher education is recognized by all to be in crisis. It is overregulated and underregulated at the same time. Bureaucracy governs virtually every aspect of college and university decision making and management, while at the same time effective quality assurance is largely missing. Except for the Indian Institutes of Technology, the Indian Institutes of Management, and a few other specialized institutions, no high-quality sector exists in Indian higher education. At the same time, the postsecondary system is unable to cater to growing demand for access, and it does not adequately serve the students who manage to gain entry.

Several proposals for expansion and reform have been put forward recently. These include proposals to open India's higher education environment to foreign investment and collaboration. After many years of keeping foreign institutions out, Indian authorities want to open up the system to create more access and opportunity for students and bring in new ideas about curriculum, organization, and reform from abroad. While much discussion has taken place in India in recent years about the regulatory framework for permitting foreign involvement in Indian higher education, no action has been taken because of political disagreements within the ruling coalition government. The recent elections and a new education minister more favorable to international involvement have changed the climate.

Potential American Involvement

There is much interest in the United States concerning Indian higher education. Many American university leaders have visited their Indian counterparts looking for potential partners for a wide range of initiatives. It is probably fair to say that India is generally seen as the second most important potential market for American higher education—China being the first—and many see China as saturated with foreign programs and initiatives. The motives of American institutions vary. Top-ranking universities wish to pursue research partnerships, the possibility of recruiting the best Indian postgraduate and undergraduate students to the home campus, and perhaps joint-degree programs of various kinds. These institutions also are seeking locations that can provide facilities and educational programs for American study-abroad students.

Lower-prestige U.S. institutions as well as some top schools are interested in India as a market for educational programs, including branch campuses, joint degrees, and the like. In some cases, overseas programs are required for financial survival—especially for smaller private institutions that face enrollment declines. Budget cuts at home are also an incentive to look for new overseas sources of revenue. The for-profit higher education sector looks to India because it offers a lucrative market for degree programs of all kinds. Some for-profits may wish to open their own campuses in India, while others may seek to partner with an existing Indian institution.

Another category of offshore academic programs is degree programs that are franchised to an Indian provider, in which the foreign partner provides the curriculum and other aspects of the academic program and oversees the program's delivery. The Indian partner, a college or university or perhaps a business firm, actually delivers the program. The degree or certificate awarded is in the name of the American institution. Some have labeled this strategy "McDonaldization," since the arrangement—licensing a product to be offered—is exactly the same as that used by the McDonald's Corporation or other franchisers.

<u>Prospects</u>

The future is potentially bright for Indo-American higher education relations. Americans recognize India as a key market for higher education. They also want to understand India's complex culture and new economic strength. India requires increased higher education capacity and new ideas to reform an underperforming academic system. Yet, there are concerns. India still requires an effective and transparent regulatory environment for foreign higher education involvement. Its quality assurance arrangements must take into account overseas participation as well as domestic institutions—building on a framework that is seen to need improvement. American accreditors must monitor U.S. institutions operating in India and ensure that appropriate standards are being maintained. Both countries want to ensure that the public good is being served by expanded Indo-American higher education involvement. If these conditions can be achieved, Indo-U.S. higher education involvement can benefit both countries.

Indo-U.S. Educational Exchange: A View from India

AJIT MOTWANI, DIRECTOR, IIE/INDIA

India is the cradle of the human race, the birthplace of human speech, the mother of history, the grandmother of legend and the great grandmother of tradition.

Mark Twain, 1835–1910

Mark Twain, the famous American writer, like many other peripatetic travellers of his generation, knew that the best education is often acquired by crossing borders and learning about different cultures. Twain's world travels between 1891 and 1901 took him to India, a country that in ancient times was a thriving center for higher education and a destination for scholars from all across the world. Even today, educational exchanges remain the most significant vehicle for cultural learning and sharing societal values, although now more than ever such mobility is also propelled by the forces of globalization and an economic and professional imperative to learn about the rest of the world.

Post-World War II educational partnerships between India and the U.S. were launched on February 2, 1950, with an agreement to facilitate the administration of the Fulbright program in India, which resulted in the establishment of the United States Educational Foundation in India (USEFI), recently renamed the United States-India Educational Foundation (USIEF). There have been several partnerships since then, the most notable being the one that led to the establishment in 1960 of the Indian Institute of Technology (IIT) at Kanpur, for which the Government of India received critical U.S. support to set up a premier institution involving a consortium of several top U.S. institutions including MIT, Princeton University, the University of California, Berkeley, and Purdue University, as well as multilateral agencies and foundations such as USAID and the Ford Foundation.

In recent times, the U.S. has been and remains a preferred destination for higher education and research for Indian students and scholars going abroad, a trend that has been of mutual benefit to both nations. While this mobility has helped India's development by providing U.S.-trained scientists and engineers who today occupy key positions in important sectors of India's knowledge economy, it has also contributed significantly to maintaining America's preeminence in the frontiers of science, technology, management, and medicine, as Vivek Wadhwa points out in his chapter for this book.

According to current estimates, over 103,000 Indian students have chosen the U.S. as their higher education destination despite America's considerable geographic distance from home. Indian students are drawn to the U.S. first and foremost for the high quality of its educational institutions but also because of their comfort with the English language and the cultural familiarity fostered by the large Indian diaspora that already exists in the United States: there are currently 3 million people of Indian origin living in the U.S., and they constitute one of the fastest growing minority groups in the country.

Although there still exists a large gap between the number of Indian students in the U.S. and the number of American students who come to India to study, it is encouraging that there is now increasing in-bound mobility *to* India. While U.S. students and scholars have traditionally been attracted to India for its unique strength in fields such as Yoga, Ayurveda, traditional visual and performing arts, classical and folk music, religion, and Gandhian studies, newer areas of study include public health, environmental studies, business management, and science and engineering—the last two being fields in which India is a world leader. And last but not the least, studying in India provides U.S. students with a valuable opportunity to experience a culture significantly different from their own and to absorb first hand the sheer breadth of India's diversity.

The growing academic mobility between the U.S. and India is due in no small part to the recent boom in the Indian economy, a success story of a developing nation on a sharp trajectory of sustained growth of over 6.5 percent even during the global downturn. This, coupled with the fact that the rapidly expanding Indian middle class places high priority on providing its children with the best available education, presents a timely opportunity to invest in and partner with the Indian education sector.

But the reverse side of the story of India's phenomenal growth is that the country has a population of over 600 million under 25 years of age, a group that is not only India's greatest asset but that also has the potential to become a liability unless it is adequately educated and trained to succeed in today's knowledge economy and globalized world. With over 60 percent of the population below 25 years and less than 12 percent of the relevant age group having access to higher education (with an even smaller proportion having access to quality education), India needs to provide quality higher education to reap the demographic benefits of a young population.

At the time of its independence from the British in 1947, India had only about 20 universities and 500 colleges. Although that number has today grown to over 400 universities and 21,000 colleges, making India's higher education system one of the largest in the world, only a small number of select Indian institutions are able to offer a high-quality education. This is, in part, why UNESCO has estimated that over 150,000 Indian students travel abroad each year to meet their educational needs. At the same time, new technologies and approaches such as information and communication technology (ICT) and distance education are being harnessed to provide educational access to large numbers of students, especially those who are unable to afford a private or an overseas education.

Despite these existing challenges, recent positive changes in India point to a new era of higher education development for the country, which will be accomplished not just through mechanisms such as domestic public-private partnerships in education but will also rely on various forms of international partnerships such as twinning, exchanges, internships, and the presence of credible foreign providers. With the appointment of a new government in 2009, there has been a renewed focus on implementing many of the educational reforms that were proposed by India's National Knowledge Commission, a high-level advisory group instituted by Prime Minister Manmohan Singh to prepare a blue print for transforming India into a vibrant knowledge society. Many of these proposed reforms, especially those involving international partnerships and foreign providers, have built upon earlier efforts by the University Grants Commission and EdCIL, which have both worked to promote India as a higher education destination.

With emerging educational destinations in Europe, Asia, and the Middle East focusing on forging educational collaborations to attract the young talent of a newly liberalized India, this is an opportune time to reemphasize the importance of higher education exchange between the U.S. and India and to further leverage the relationship that has evolved between the two democracies over the last 60 years. U.S.-India relations are the best ever in the history of the two nations, and our IIE/AIFS book offers unique and hitherto unexplored perspectives on the challenges, opportunities, and modalities of furthering higher education partnerships between the two countries.

This book calls upon the perspectives of experts working in different areas of international education to address the U.S.-India exchange relationship. To provide a context for the chapters that follow, Rajika Bhandari and Rahul Choudaha in their opening chapter examine data on higher education mobility between the U.S. and India, situating these trends within the larger context of the diversification of U.S.-India education partnerships. The second chapter by Alina Romanowski, Deputy Assistant Secretary of State for Academic Programs, U.S. Department of State, Bureau of Educational and Cultural Affairs, describes the many State Department initiatives that promote U.S.-India exchanges. In a parallel chapter, Sam Pitroda, a leading figure in India's technology revolution and the former head of the country's National Knowledge Commission, shares the commission's national-level recommendations for promoting U.S.-India exchange.

Keeping the focus on developments in India, Pawan Agarwal looks specifically at the internationalization of the Indian higher education system, providing an in-depth analysis of factors that influence India's inbound and outbound mobility. Agarwal introduces the topic of foreign providers in India, and the following chapter by Sudhanshu Bhushan looks at the politics and economics of allowing increased operations by foreign education providers in India—a subject that has received significant attention recently in India and abroad.

The next few chapters explore Indo-U.S. higher education exchanges from the viewpoint of U.S. institutions, students, and the American workforce. In his analysis of successful Indian entrepreneurs in the U.S., Vivek Wadhwa, an entrepreneur-turned-academic and executive in residence at the Center for Entrepreneurship and Research Commercialization at Duke University, traces the contributions that Indian students and alumni have made to U.S. competitiveness, especially in the fields of science and technology. Also focusing on students rather than institutional initiatives, Darla Deardorff and her Indian colleagues examine the development of intercultural competence as an important outcome of U.S.-India exchanges. Nicole Ranganath describes the evolution of the University of California-India Initiative and the successful partnerships and best practices that emerged as a result. In an interview with IIE, Krishna Vedula of the University of Massachusetts Lowell provides his perspectives on how various recent developments in India, in particular the proposed Indian legislation on regulations for foreign providers, would affect the future of Indo-U.S. educational partnerships.

Finally, we offer a concluding essay by P.J. Lavakare, currently a member of the Board of Management at Symbiosis International University, reflecting on the developments that have occurred during his many years as a participant in the U.S.-India exchange relationship. We hope that the book will make a significant contribution to this new and optimistic phase in Indo-U.S. higher education relations.

Chapter One

U.S.-India Mobility at a Turning Point: Background and Trends

Rajika Bhandari, Director, Research and Evaluation,
Institute of International Education

Rahul Choudaha, Associate Director of Development and Innovation,
World Education Services

Despite their social, cultural and demographic differences, India and the United States share important commonalities when it comes to their higher education systems. India was home to ancient centers of learning, like Takshila (700 BC) and Nalanda University (400 AD), that attracted scholars from countries such as Greece and China; today, the U.S. is widely regarded as the world leader in higher education. Also, in terms of size and number of institutions, the Indian and U.S. higher education systems are today among the three largest systems in the world, with U.S. higher education enrollments far exceeding those of India. Another common feature is that the language of instruction in both countries is English, and this is perhaps one of the major reasons that Indian students have eagerly sought educational opportunity in the United States, coupled with America's strength in science and technology graduate education.

While the U.S. has attracted thousands of Indian students over the years, India is beginning to emerge as a higher education destination in its own right. This rise in international students in India may not match the large numbers of Indian students going abroad, but it is nevertheless an encouraging trend. There are many indicators that India is poised to play an increasingly important role in global higher education mobility—not just as one of the world's largest consumers of international education but also as an increasingly important provider of such education. The rapid growth of its economy and the emergence of a consumer-driven middle class have resulted in greater demand for quality higher education, whether at home or abroad.

But despite this sense of optimism about the country's growth, significant challenges persist in the field of education. With one of the world's largest higher education systems, comprised of more than 400 universities and 21,000 colleges, India not only faces severe limitations in providing its own college-aged population with high-quality, adequate opportunities for higher education, but it has also attracted only a modest number of international students, mostly because the system only includes a small base of quality institutions for graduate studies and research. Even so, the country still manages to attract international students from about 125 countries for various undergraduate, graduate, and research programs (Agarwal, 2008).

The U.S., on the other hand, is one of the world's most technologically and economically advanced countries, and it has no shortage of good facilities for higher education and training. Yet there is serious concern in the U.S. higher education community that not enough of its students participate in international learning experiences and, as a result, lack cultural knowledge, understanding, and global competitiveness, which can best be acquired through overseas study. These concerns have led to a strong push in the U.S. international education community to invest the necessary resources at the national, state, and institutional levels to send more U.S. students abroad. Indeed, U.S. study abroad has increased at a steady pace of approximately 8 percent annually over the past several years, and all indications suggest that this trend will continue.

A particularly encouraging aspect of this growth is that American students are increasingly selecting what might be considered "nontraditional" higher education destinations—countries outside Western Europe and Australia—which often have vastly different cultures, languages, and educational systems. India has figured as one such nontraditional destination and has been among the top 25 destinations for U.S. study abroad since 2005/06 (Bhandari & Chow, 2010). Moreover, the number of U.S. students going to India for a study abroad experience increased by over 300 percent in just the past decade. These trends point to a new era in Indo-U.S. higher education mobility.

Our chapter is divided into three main sections. Co-author Rajika Bhandari opens with a discussion of U.S.-bound trends; that is, the numbers of Indian students and faculty that have participated in U.S. higher education over the past several decades. This is followed by a section that explores the reverse trend, which is on the rise: U.S. students and scholars in India. The data presented in these two sections come primarily from *Open Doors*, the Institute of International Education's flagship research project, which is supported by the U.S. Department of State and focuses on trends in international educational exchange between the U.S. and other countries. Data from the Fulbright program is also presented, as it is America's most important program for facilitating postsecondary exchanges and mobility between the U.S. and other nations. The final portion of the chapter, by coauthor Rahul Choudaha, takes a more qualitative approach, focusing on the existing educational partnerships between the U.S. and India that will prove to be critical in driving Indo-U.S. mobility trends in the future.

Indian Students and Scholars in the U.S.

Ever since Indian students and immigrants began to arrive in the U.S. in the late 1940s, America has been one of the most popular destinations for Indian students seeking higher education outside their own country. The presence of Indian students in the U.S. has grown since the mid-1950s, with Indian students in the U.S. surpassing Chinese students in 2001/02. The number of students from India increased steadily between 1996/97 and 2004/05, then declined by 5 percent in 2005/06. Since then the number has grown steadily, reaching 103,260 students in 2008/09 (figure 1.1).

Over the past decade (1998/99 to 2008/09), enrollments from India have grown by 37 percent. Despite this positive growth, there are indications that enrollments from India at U.S. institutions for the 2009/10 academic year may see either declines at certain academic levels or, at the very least, slower rates of growth. Recently released international enrollment data by the Council of Graduate Schools (CGS) shows a 4 percent decline in total enrollment among Indian graduate students and a 16 percent decline among newly enrolled Indian graduate students for the 2009/10 academic year (CGS, 2009). Additionally, F-1 (student) visas issued in India between October 2008 and September 2009 declined by 25 percent. But the picture is more complex than these numbers suggest: although there may have been declines in offers of admission to Indian graduate students and corresponding declines in enrollment, some top institutions saw increases. Also, undergraduate international enrollments in the U.S. have surged, and it is quite possible that these increases might offset any declines seen at the graduate level.

FIGURE 1.1: INDIAN STUDENTS IN THE U.S., 1948/49 TO 2008/09

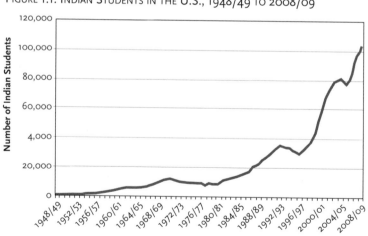

Source: Bhandari, R., & Chow, P. (2010). *Open doors 2009: Report on international educational exchange.* New York, NY: Institute of International Education.

Most Indian students in the U.S. (69 percent) are enrolled in graduate-level programs, with a much smaller proportion pursuing undergraduate study (15 percent) or other types of programs (such as nondegree and intensive English programs). Most Indians on U.S. campuses are enrolled in business and management and in the fields of science, technology, engineering, and mathematics (STEM), which has allowed them to make significant contributions to U.S. competitiveness in science and technology. Like most international students in the U.S., Indian students are drawn to universities in the urban areas of large states such as California, Texas, New York, Illinois, and Pennsylvania, all of which also have large Indian diaspora communities. Table 1.1 lists, in descending order, the top 15 U.S. institutions that hosted Indian students in 2008/09.

TABLE 1.1: TOP 15 U.S. INSTITUTIONS HOSTING INDIAN STUDENTS, 2008/09 (ALPHABETICAL)

Rank	Institution	City	State
1	University of Southern California	Los Angeles	California
2	University of Bridgeport	Bridgeport	Connecticut
3	Purdue University - Main Campus	West Lafayette	Indiana
4	University of Texas - Arlington	Arlington	Texas
5	Illinois Institute of Technology	Chicago	Illinois
6	SUNY University at Buffalo	Buffalo	New York
7	University of Florida	Gainesville	Florida
8	Texas A&M University	College Station	Texas
9	University of Texas - Dallas	Richardson	Texas
10	Arizona State University - Tempe Campus	Tempe	Arizona
11	San Jose State University	San Jose	California
12	Georgia Institute of Technology	Atlanta	Georgia
13	Carnegie Mellon University	Pittsburgh	Pennsylvania
14	North Carolina State University	Raleigh	North Carolina
15	University of Michigan - Ann Arbor	Ann Arbor	Michigan

Source: Bhandari, R., & Chow, P. (2010). *Open doors 2009: Report on international educational exchange.* New York, NY: Institute of International Education.

Indian Fulbright Students in the U.S.

The Fulbright fellowship program for students from India has typically focused on predoctoral research and nondegree study. Since 1992, approximately 380 Indian students have come to the U.S. on Fulbright fellowships. More recently, the new Fulbright Master's Fellowships for Leadership Development program, initiated in 2005 and administered by the United States-India Education Foundation (USIEF), targets master's-level candidates and has awarded 55 fellowships in the past 17 years, representing approximately 15 percent of the total number of Fulbright awards made to Indian students. The number of master's-level candidates for the fellowship is expected to continue to increase over the coming years. In terms of gender, women have made up 38 percent of the Indian Fulbright student population since 1992.

Most Fulbright students from India are enrolled in the field of business. However, this concentration is primarily due to a special USIEF program sponsored by the Confederation of Indian Industries (CII). This program, "Leadership for Management," is a short-term certificate for business professionals. Other popular fields of study have included literature, law, arts, and communications; overall, literature has been the most popular field for grantees over the past 17 years of the program.

Indian Students' Perceptions of the U.S. as a Destination

A recent IIE study carried out in fall 2009 examined the attitudes and perceptions of the U.S. among 1,044 prospective international students from India. It is the second report in a series of attitudinal surveys of students from key sending countries. Students were surveyed on their preferred study abroad destinations, their reasons for studying abroad, the major obstacles they faced and their main sources of information on study abroad as well as their opinions of the U.S. as a potential study abroad destination compared to five other common host destinations. Key findings include the following:

- The U.S. is the destination of choice for the majority of respondents, with 97 percent reporting the U.S. as either their first- or second-choice study abroad destination;

- The U.S. is perceived to have the highest quality higher education system and widest range of schools and programs compared to the United Kingdom, Australia, Continental Europe, Southeast/East Asia, and the Middle East, as well as being a safe place to study which welcomes international students and offers a good lifestyle, good student support services, and many scholarships opportunities;

- Cost was cited as the primary obstacle to study abroad.

Overall, the survey results indicate that the positioning of the United States as a potential study abroad destination for Indian students is currently very strong compared to other possible destinations. Respondents in all four major Indian cities overwhelmingly chose the United States as their first-choice destination for study abroad, with second- and third-place United Kingdom and Canada only garnering single-digit percentages. Among respondents who did not select the United States as their first-choice destination, almost 70 percent did select it as their second-choice destination. Less that 3 percent of respondents listed the United States as neither their first- nor second-choice study abroad destination.

The survey results also revealed several strengths and weaknesses for the United States as a study abroad destination for students from India. Most respondents cited the quality or type of academic programs as their main reason for wishing to study abroad. Compared to the United Kingdom, Australia, Continental Europe, Southeast/East Asia and the Middle East, the United States was rated the most highly for its excellent higher education system and wide range of schools and programs, as well as for being welcoming toward international students, offering a good lifestyle, and for being a safe place to study. However, the United States received the poorest ratings for the cost of tuition, cost of school application process, and distance from home. Furthermore, only the United Kingdom was perceived to have more difficult or complicated visa procedures. Addressing these issues will ensure that the United States remains the premier destination for students from India who wish to pursue higher education in another country.

Indian Scholars in the U.S.

As in the case of Indian students, Indian scholars have come to the U.S. in increasing numbers to pursue teaching and research at U.S. institutions (figure 1.2). India has ranked among the top five places of origin for America's international scholars since 1989. According to the most current data available through *Open Doors*, 10,814 Indian scholars were present on U.S. campuses in 2008/09, a 9 percent increase over the previous year, which places India as the second largest country of origin of international scholars in the U.S., after China.

FIGURE 1.2: INTERNATIONAL SCHOLARS FROM INDIA IN THE U.S., 1989/90 TO 2008/09

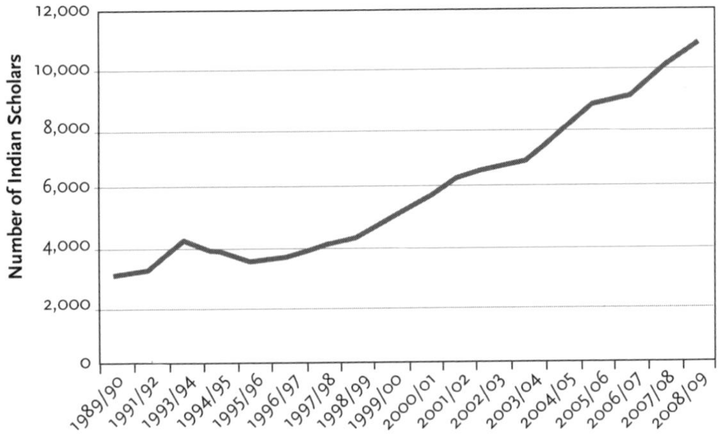

Source: Bhandari, R., & Chow, P. (2010). *Open doors 2009: Report on international educational exchange.* New York, NY: Institute of International Education.

Indian Fulbright Scholars in the U.S.

The Fulbright Scholar Program is a popular pathway for Indian scholars to come to the U.S. and for U.S. faculty to visit Indian institutions. Since 1994, approximately 265 Indian scholars have come to the U.S. on the Fulbright program. More recently,

Fulbright Visiting Scholars from India have been coming to the U.S. in increasing numbers to teach. In the mid-1990s, 79 percent of Visiting Scholars from India came on research grants, and only 20 percent on teaching grants (the remaining 1 percent combined teaching and research). Between 2004 and 2008, however, only 56 percent of Visiting Scholars came from India on research grants, 38 percent came on teaching grants, and 6 percent combined teaching and research. This is *not* part of a worldwide shift: overall, slightly over 80 percent of Fulbright Visiting Scholars have come to the U.S. to conduct research, both in the past and in the last five years.

Over the last 15 years (1994–2008), teaching-centered institutions in the U.S. have become more involved with the Fulbright Scholar Program both to and from India. While most Visiting Scholars from India are still affiliated with large doctoral/research institutions, the percentage affiliated with master's and baccalaureate institutions has increased from 3 to 15 percent and from 0 to 3 percent, respectively.

In recent years, Visiting Fulbright Scholars from India have been less likely to conduct research and teach in the STEM fields, which is particularly unusual in view of the high proportion of STEM scholars among international scholars in general. Between 1994 and 1998, 35 percent of all scholars from India were in the STEM fields, compared with 24 percent between 2004 and 2008. Within the STEM fields, Visiting Scholars have been less concentrated in the fields of biology, chemistry, and physics, which dominated the mid-1990s, and particularly in the last five years have concentrated much more heavily on environmental science and agriculture. In the mid-1990s, the top fields for Visiting Scholars from India were (in descending order) economics, political science, and American literature. During the last five years, the top fields have been education, environmental science, and political science.

U.S. Students and Scholars in India

Although the U.S. has always been a favored destination for Indian students seeking an international education, India has only recently begun to attract increasing numbers of U.S. students and faculty. According to the most current estimates available from *Open Doors*, approximately 3,200 U.S. students studied in India in 2007/08, a 20 percent increase over the previous year, making India the 17th most popular study abroad destination among the top 20 destinations for U.S. study-abroad students. These figures, from the *Open Doors* U.S. study abroad survey, do not include U.S. students who have enrolled directly in an Indian institution for degree study. Hence, the total number of U.S. students enrolled in Indian institutions might be slightly higher than the number reported here. Over time, the number of study abroad students to India has gone up from 684 in 1997/98 to 3,146 in 2007/08, an increase of 360 percent over the past 11 years (figure 1.3).

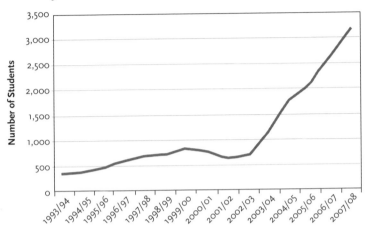

Source: Bhandari, R., & Chow, P. (2010). *Open doors 2009: Report on international educational exchange.* New York, NY: Institute of International Education.

The increase in U.S. study abroad to India has been fueled by American students seeking nontraditional study abroad destinations, but it is also partly due to India's overall growth as a higher education destination. A number of national-level efforts have been underway in India to attract more international students and scholars, which include increasing the flexibility of the Indian higher education curricula and structure. These efforts have enabled more students from other countries to study in India. There were 18,594 international students enrolled in India's higher education system in 2007, a 40 percent increase since 2005 (Project Atlas, 2009). Most international students in India are from developing countries in the neighboring regions of South Asia and the Middle East. In 2007, the U.S. ranked 7th among the top 10 sending countries, accounting for approximately 3 percent of all international students in India.

But despite the recent growth in U.S. study abroad to India, there remains a significant educational exchange imbalance between the two countries: there were only 3,146 U.S. students in India in 2007/08 as compared with 103,260 Indian students enrolled in U.S. institutions in 2008/09 (figure 1.4). The imbalance is further exacerbated by the length of time students spend in each others' institutions, with Indians coming to the U.S. for degree study, often at the PhD level, while U.S. students usually go to India for short-term study or a semester at most. This large gap points to the need to expand partnerships between U.S. and Indian institutions with the goal of increasing faculty and student exchanges, a topic we explore in the last section of this chapter.

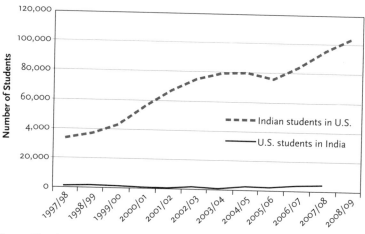

FIGURE 1.4: EDUCATIONAL EXCHANGE BALANCE BETWEEN INDIA AND THE U.S., 1997/98 TO 2008/09

Source: Bhandari, R., & Chow, P. (2010). *Open doors 2009: Report on international educational exchange.* New York, NY: Institute of International Education.

U.S. Institutions that Send Students to India

While U.S. students going to India for study abroad come from the full spectrum of U.S. higher education institutions, most are undergraduates who attend doctorate/research institutions (figure 1.5). Significant proportions of students also attend U.S. master's and baccalaureate institutions (15 and 22 percent, respectively). Table 1.2 lists, in descending order, the top 15 U.S. institutions that sent students to India.

FIGURE 1.5: U.S. STUDENTS IN INDIA BY TYPE OF SENDING INSTITUTION, 2007/08

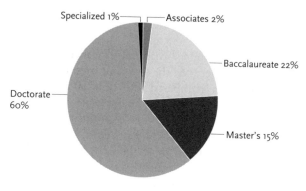

Source: Bhandari, R., & Chow, P. (2010). *Open doors 2009: Report on international educational exchange.* New York, NY: Institute of International Education.

Institution	City	State
College of Saint Catherine	Saint Paul	Minnesota
Cornell University	Ithaca	New York
Georgetown University	Washington	District of Columbia
Indiana University - Bloomington	Bloomington	Indiana
Michigan State University	East Lansing	Michigan
Purdue University - Main Campus	West Lafayette	Indiana
Temple University	Philadelphia	Pennsylvania
University of Arkansas - Main Campus	Fayetteville	Arkansas
University of Iowa	Iowa City	Iowa
University of Michigan - Ann Arbor	Ann Arbor	Michigan
University of Minnesota - Twin Cities	Minneapolis	Minnesota
University of Pennsylvania	Philadelphia	Pennsylvania
University of Saint Thomas	Houston	Texas
University of Washington	Seattle	Washington
University of Wisconsin - Madison	Madison	Wisconsin

Source: Bhandari, R., & Chow, P. (2010). *Open doors 2009: Report on international educational exchange.* New York, NY: Institute of International Education.

U.S. Scholars in India

In general, scarce data are available on the worldwide mobility of U.S. scholars and faculty, primarily because such information is difficult to collect. Faculty often undertake overseas research or teaching assignments independently and are not required to coordinate their activities through an on-campus office at their U.S. institution. Therefore, the data presented in this section focus on structured mobility programs, like the Fulbright program, that collect data on participating U.S. and foreign scholars.

Between 1994 and 2008, close to 400 U.S. faculty conducted research in India or taught at Indian institutions as part of the Fulbright program. Some similar trends can be observed between Indian Fulbright Scholars in the U.S. and American scholars going to India: over the last 15 years, teaching-centered institutions in the U.S. have become more involved with the Fulbright Scholar Program both to and from India. The percentage of U.S. Fulbright Scholars to India coming from master's institutions has increased from 10 percent to 26 percent, while the percentage of those coming from baccalaureate institutions has increased from 9 percent to 11 percent. The percentage of those coming from doctoral institutions in the U.S. has decreased from 72 percent to 46 percent; the remaining grantees are independent scholars or come from public or private agencies.

But there are also contrasting trends. Unlike their Indian colleagues coming to America, U.S. Fulbright Scholars to India have been increasingly involved in the STEM fields: between 2004 and 2008, 31 percent of scholars to India were specialists in the

STEM fields, as compared with 21 percent between 1994 and 1998. The top fields for U.S. Fulbright Scholars to India in the mid-1990s were (in descending order) art, sociology, American literature, and anthropology. The top fields during the last five years have been business administration, engineering, and medical sciences.

The gender balance among Fulbright Scholars both to and from India has improved. While during the mid-1990s male scholars typically outnumbered female scholars by more than two to one, in the last five years a male/female ratio of 55 percent to 45 percent has been more typical.

Higher Education Partnerships between U.S. and Indian Institutions

Higher education partnerships between India and the U.S. have grown in scale and scope along with increasing political and economic interaction between the two countries. For example, in the late 1990s, the emergence of knowledge-based sectors like information technology services in India resulted in knowledge and service exchange along with talent mobility to the United States. Likewise, there has been a sense of optimism about the growth and impact of India on the global economy.

This transformation of the Indian economy resulted in increasing interest within the management and engineering disciplines in participating in this growth and integrating it with their academic and research offerings. Thus, engineering and management disciplines are among the most popular for education partnerships, although other fields like agriculture, medicine, and biotechnology have also attracted attention.

Academic and research exchange between India and the U.S. dates back to the early 1960s, when post-independence India was seeking to improve its higher education system in line with changing technological and economic conditions. India's premier technical and management institutions—the Indian Institutes of Technology (IIT) and Indian Institutes of Management (IIM)—were established with the support of leading American universities. For example, IIM Calcutta was established in 1961 as the first national institute for graduate-level education and research in management by the Government of India, in collaboration with the Alfred P. Sloan School of Management (MIT), the Government of West Bengal, The Ford Foundation, and Indian industry (IIM Calcutta, 2008). Likewise, during the period 1960–72, IIT Kanpur received technical assistance, under the Kanpur Indo-American Programme (KIAP), from a consortium of nine leading American institutions including Princeton University, California Institute of Technology, and MIT. This support involved setting up academic and research programs at the new institutions, including procurement of equipment, books, and journals not available in India (IIT Kanpur, 2007).

This section of the chapter, by coauthor Rahul Choudaha, is divided into three subsections. The first section covers academic exchanges, the second focuses on research collaborations, and the third and final section highlights the role of foundations, grants and fellowships, and India studies in U.S.-India exchanges.

Academic Exchange: Joint Degree/Dual Degree/Twinning Programs

Academic exchange between India and the U.S. can be grouped into two primary categories—short-term/semester-length study abroad programs and joint degree, dual degree or twinning programs. The terms "joint degree," "dual degree," and "twinning programs" are often used interchangeably to indicate forms of academic collaboration between two institutions in which the student receives a single jointly signed certificate or two separate certificates upon completion of the program. India's higher education system is one of the most highly regulated systems in the world; thus, the establishment of foreign universities and programs is constrained by existing regulatory processes. Given the regulatory constraints faced by U.S. institutions in their efforts to establish full-fledged campuses and the continued interest among Indian students in gaining U.S. academic credentials, twinning programs have become very popular (Neelakantan, 2008). Under a typical U.S.-India twinning program, a student spends the first two years of the academic program in India and then transfers to a U.S. partner institution. Twinning arrangements are quite popular, as they involve the least risk for foreign institutions and offer a predictable revenue stream (Neelakantan, 2008). Table 1.3 lists some existing twinning arrangements.

Manipal University offers one of the most comprehensive twinning programs in India through the International Center for Applied Sciences (ICAS), which provides a four-year twinning program in engineering: students pursue the first two years of the program at Manipal and the subsequent years with the U.S. partner university. Since ICAS was started in 1994, over 900 students have graduated through this twinning arrangement. In such an arrangement, curriculum mapping for proper credit transfers is critical. The U.S. partner universities for Manipal ICAS are Andrews University, Illinois Institute of Technology, Michigan Technological University, Milwaukee School of Engineering, St. Cloud State University, the University of Missouri-Kansas City, North Dakota State University, and the University of Miami.

Likewise, Ansal Institute of Technology at Gurgaon has also established twinning arrangements with several U.S. universities, including North Dakota State University, Clemson University, Eastern Michigan University, San Jose State University, North Carolina State University, New Jersey Institute of Technology, and Valparaiso University.

Amrita University in Bangalore and the State University of New York (SUNY) at Buffalo offer a program that allows students to earn two master's degrees in management. One is an MBA degree from Amrita University in general management, and the other is a Master of Science in Management of Information Technology Services from the SUNY Buffalo.

Another example is the Purdue University partnership with Cummins College of Engineering for Women (CCEW), Pune. Under this arrangement, CCEW bachelor's degree graduates get an opportunity to pursue master's and doctoral studies at

Purdue's West Lafayette campus. It also involves collaboration in the areas of research and development, as well as student and faculty exchanges.

Champlain College in Vermont offers accredited two-year associate's and four-year bachelor's degrees in business, hospitality industry management, and software engineering through St. Xavier's Technical Institute, Mumbai.

TABLE 1.3: JOINT DEGREE/DUAL DEGREE/TWINNING PROGRAMS

Amrita University, Bangalore and the University at Buffalo, New York (SUNY)
http://mites.amrita.edu
Ansal Institute of Technology at Gurgaon
www.aitgurgaon.org/AboutUs/AcademicLinkages1.html
Christ University, Bangalore, and Western Michigan University
www.christuniversity.in/display_article.php?fid=23&arid=14
Cummins College of Engineering for Women (CCEW), Pune, and Purdue University
http://news.uns.purdue.edu/x/2008b/081117CordovaTrip.html
Lal Bahadur Shastri Institute of Management, Delhi, and Southwest Missouri State University
www.lbsim.ac.in/About/international_collaboration.html
Manipal University
www.manipal.edu/manipalsite/users/Colsubpage.aspx?PgId=582&ID=1&collegeId=24
Tamil Nadu Agricultural University (TNAU), Coimbatore, India, and Cornell University
www.news.cornell.edu/stories/Feb09/IndiaMPS.kr.html
St. Xavier's Technical Institute, Mumbai, and Champlain College, Burlington, Vermont
http://extra.champlain.edu/international/satellites/india/index.php

Business schools have been proactive in forging alliances and offering joint programs where students receive a co-signed certificate of completion from all partner universities (table 1.4). It is important to note that these credentials are not approved by the Indian education regulator and hence are not "joint degrees" in the formal sense of the term. They have, however, gained significant acceptance from students, industry, and U.S. partner institutions.

A pioneer in the field of joint certificate programs, the Indian School of Business (ISB) offers one of the most highly regarded business programs in India. It offers a one-year postgraduate program in management in partnership with the Wharton School at the University of Pennsylvania, the Kellogg School of Management at Northwestern University, and the London Business School (LBS). As table 1.4 shows, other schools have also adopted the successful ISB model of joint programs.

TABLE 1.4: JOINT ACADEMIC PROGRAMS AT BUSINESS SCHOOLS

Asia Graduate School of Business, Hyderabad, and Fisher College of Business at Ohio State University www.asiagsb.ac.in
Indian School of Business, Hyderabad; the Wharton School at the University of Pennsylvania; the Kellogg School of Management at Northwestern University ; and London Business School www.isb.edu
Great Lakes Institute of Management, Chennai; Illinois Institute of Technology; Yale University; and Nanyang Technological University, Singapore www.greatlakes.edu.in
National Management School, Chennai, and J. Mack Robinson College of Business, Georgia State University www.nms.edu.in

Research Collaborations

The evolution of the Indian economy towards globalization, technology, and knowledge-based services has had an influence on higher education and research in India, including its relationship with the United States. International research collaborations have become a key channel in gaining competitiveness in the global knowledge economy (Hatakenaka, 2008). At one level, international research collaborations provide deep insights about the partner country and institution, and at another level they aid in building a complementary research base. To this end, several U.S. and Indian academic institutions have proactively engaged in research collaborations that have taken place in a range of disciplines, including management, engineering, biotechnology, science, and agriculture (table 1.5).

TABLE 1.5: RESEARCH COLLABORATIONS

Amrita University www.amrita.edu/indo-us/media.html
Berkeley-India Joint Leadership on Energy and Environment (BIJLEE) http://india.lbl.gov/pdf/bijlee-description.pdf
Great Lakes Institute of Management and Yale University www.greatlakes.edu.in/introduction.php#
Indian Institute of Technology (IIT), Kharagpur, and the University of California, San Diego http://ucsdnews.ucsd.edu/newsrel/health/08-09IITKGP.asp
Purdue University https://engineering.purdue.edu/Engr/AboutUs/News/Publications/EngineeringImpact/2007_1/PurduesIndianResearchNetwork
U.S.-India Agricultural Knowledge Initiative (AKI) www.fas.usda.gov/icd/india_knowl_init/india_knowl_init.asp

Within the management field, Great Lakes Institute of Management, Chennai, partnered with Yale University to establish Yale-Great Lakes Center for Management Research, which conducts management research with a focus on India and contributes to the development of basic and applied knowledge in the field. In engineering and science, the Berkeley-India Joint Leadership on Energy and Environment (BIJLEE) is a partnership in the area of energy management and sustainable economic development. The BIJLEE partners include the University of California, Berkeley (UC Berkeley), the Lawrence Berkeley National Laboratory (Berkeley Lab), the governments of the United States and India, and educational institutions and industry partners in the two countries.

In the field of agriculture, the U.S.-India Knowledge Initiative on Agricultural Education, Teaching, Research, Service, and Commercial Linkages (AKI) addresses new challenges and opportunities related to environmentally sustainable, market-oriented agriculture. It engages academia, government, and private sector representatives from the United States and India. For example, 15 Indian scientists and researchers completed USDA fellowships, and APLU awarded five grants to U.S. universities to work with Indian partners on various aspects of capacity building.

In August 2009, IIT Kharagpur and the University of California, San Diego, announced an extensive relationship in health sciences covering research, academics, and administrative services. The plan includes establishing a collaborative 300-bed hospital where UC San Diego will provide leadership and training in all aspects of hospital administration. The research and development program will include faculty, student, and resident exchanges.

Another important and emerging form of collaboration is the presence of dedicated research centers established by American universities in India. For example, Harvard Business School established the India Research Center (IRC) in 2006 in Mumbai. The IRC supports the school's faculty in following the emerging trends in the region and pursuing cutting-edge research in a wide range of industries including technology, biotechnology, healthcare, agribusiness, and corporate governance (www.hbs.edu/global/research/southasia/center). Likewise, the University of Pennsylvania Institute for the Advanced Study of India (UPIASI), founded in 1997 in New Delhi, undertakes research projects and engages scholars across a range of institutions to produce research relevant to regional needs (www.sas.upenn.edu/upiasi). The Center for the Advanced Study of India at the University of Pennsylvania is a research center dedicated to the study of contemporary India (http://casi.ssc.upenn.edu).

Foundations, Grants and Fellowships, and India Studies

Foundations and nonprofits have been active in supporting research engagement between the U.S. and India. For example, the Ford Foundation established an office in India in 1952 as its first office outside the U.S., and the office remains one of its largest international field operations. The International Fellowships Program (IFP) of the Ford Foundation is especially designed to support candidates from groups that have historically lacked access to higher education in developing countries where Ford has field offices. IFP provides support for a maximum of two years of formal master's degree study and had 40 fellowships available in 2009 for Indians from marginalized communities.

In India, the USIEF administers IFP. USIEF also administers Fulbright fellowships for Indian and American students, faculty, and professionals, and offers educational advising services for students interested in pursuing higher education in the United States. USIEF was established under a bilateral agreement on educational exchange signed between India and the U.S. in 1950. In 2008, the new Fulbright agreement made India and the U.S. equal partners and doubled the annual scholarship funds.

India studies is a well-established discipline that encourages academic and research exchanges between the U.S. and India. Many of the top research universities in the U.S. have India studies centers that engage in a range of activities, including providing grants and fellowships to faculty and students visiting India (table 1.6). For example, the South Asia Initiative at Harvard University offers grants each academic year for students and faculty pursuing interests in South Asia.

The American Institute of Indian Studies (AIIS), established in 1961, is among the most active nonprofit organizations of 60 American colleges and universities that supports the advancement of knowledge and understanding of India, its people, and culture. More than 3,500 scholars have received AIIS support, and nearly 50 books related to Indian studies have been published by the institute.

TABLE 1.6: GRANTS, FELLOWSHIPS, AND INDIA STUDIES

American Institute of Indian Studies	www.indiastudies.org/fellow.htm
Cornell University	www.einaudi.cornell.edu/southasia
Ford Foundation	www.ifpsa.org
Harvard University	www.fas.harvard.edu/~sainit/grants.htm
Indian Council of Social Science Research (ICSSR)	www.icssr.org/ic_main.htm
University of California, Berkeley Center for South Asia Studies (CSAS)	http://southasia.berkeley.edu
University of Houston	www.foundationforindiastudies.org

Future Opportunities and Challenges

U.S.-India relationships have undergone significant change in scope and direction in the last decade. The changing geopolitical and economic environments in both countries have resulted in interdependencies, synergies, and gains both for India and the United States. Education exchanges are integral to strengthening these bilateral exchanges as they directly relate to human capital development and talent mobility. During her 2009 visit to India, U.S. Secretary of State Hillary Clinton remarked at the U.S.-India Business Council that "Our countries should continue the tradition of intellectual exchange by increasing opportunities for interaction by American institutions of higher learning and their Indian counterparts as well."

Leading American research universities have expressed significant interest in forging extensive partnerships with Indian institutions. In the past two years, several U.S. universities, including Cornell University, Yale University, Purdue University, and the University of California, have participated in presidential delegations to India to explore relationships with Indian institutions. Some have initiated new relationships, while others have strengthened existing ones. However, these relationships at present are far from attaining their maximum potential.

Expanding and building new partnerships between Indian and American universities is fraught with challenges. First, there is a wide spectrum of quality on both sides, and the current regulatory system in India lacks the capacity to separate the wheat from the chaff. India needs to create a more robust, transparent, and quality-conscious system of higher education that supports international education exchanges rather than hindering them.

Second, at the institutional level, both Indian and American institutions need to gain deeper insights about the context in which partner institutions operate and the level of adaptation and innovation required to make partnerships work. For example, the issue of reservations or quotas (specific percentages of seats allocated for students from underrepresented communities) may pose a barrier to the entry of American universities, which generally prefer autonomy in the admissions process. On the other hand, India is a complex and diverse nation and needs appropriate mechanisms for creating opportunities of equitable access.

Third, the existing imbalance of student mobility is a challenge—103,260 Indian students are enrolled in U.S. institutions, as compared to only 3,146 American students studying in India for short-term programs. India needs to overcome this challenge and leverage its cultural diversity and economic transformation as an opportunity to attract students. India needs to emphasize its potential as a higher education destination that provides not only wide-ranging academic offerings but also a safe and comfortable infrastructure for campus life.

While U.S.-India education exchanges have their share of challenges, future opportunities and their impact on overall relationships between the two countries far exceed these existing limitations. As Heffernan and Poole (2005) rightly conclude, creating effective international partnerships requires "… development of effective communication networks and structures, the building of trust between partners, and ongoing demonstrations of commitment to the relationship" (p. 243). Going forward, Indian and American universities need to continue to innovate, develop, and strengthen bilateral educational exchanges in a concerted manner.

REFERENCES

Agarwal, P. (2008). India in the context of international student circulation. In H. De Wit (Ed.), *The dynamics of international student circulation in a global context* (pp. 83–112). Rotterdam and Taipei: Sense Publishers.

Bhandari, R., & Chow, P. (2010). *Open doors 2009: Report on international educational exchange.* New York, NY: Institute of International Education.

Council of Graduate Schools. (2009). *Findings from the 2009 CGS international graduate admissions survey phase III: Final offers of admission and enrollment.* Retrieved from http://www.cgsnet.org/portals/0/pdf/ R_IntlEnrl09_III.pdf

Hatakenaka, S. (2008). New developments in international research collaboration. Retrieved June 17, 2009 from http://www.bc.edu/bc_org/avp/soe/cihe/newsletter/Number50/p11_Hatakenaka.htm

Heffernan, T., & Poole, D. (2005). In search of "the vibe": Creating effective international education partnerships. *Higher Education, 50*(2), 223–245.

IIM Calcutta. (2008). About IIM Calcutta. Retrieved June 14, 2009, from http://www.iimcal.ac.in/ campus/default.asp

IIT Kanpur. (2007). Kanpur Indo-American Programme (KIAP). Retrieved June 14, 2009, from http://www.iitk.ac.in/infocell/iitk/history/kiap.html

Neelakantan, S. (2008, February 8). In India, limits on foreign universities lead to creative partnerships. *The Chronicle of Higher Education, 54*(22), A1.

Project Atlas. (2009). India. Retrieved from http://www.atlas.iienetwork.org/?p=53608

Chapter Two
NATIONAL POLICY GOALS: U.S. DEPARTMENT OF STATE ACTIVITIES SUPPORTING U.S.-INDIA ACADEMIC EXCHANGES

ALINA L. ROMANOWSKI, DEPUTY ASSISTANT SECRETARY OF STATE FOR ACADEMIC PROGRAMS, U.S. DEPARTMENT OF STATE, BUREAU OF EDUCATIONAL AND CULTURAL AFFAIRS

Introduction

India is emerging as a global leader. The country is a major foreign policy priority and a crucial global partner for the United States. Recognizing the progress in the India-U.S. relationship over the last two Indian and U.S. administrations, the U.S. is committed to pursuing a third and transformative phase of the relationship that will enhance global prosperity and stability in the twenty-first century.

During her July 2009 visit to India, U.S. Secretary of State Hillary Rodham Clinton and Indian External Affairs Minister S.M. Krishna issued a joint statement regarding their intentions to accelerate the growth of their countries' bilateral relationship to enhance global prosperity and stability. The two governments outlined a Strategic Dialogue that will focus on five principal pillars, including a pillar devoted to education and development.

The United States and India agreed to strengthen existing bilateral relationships and mechanisms for cooperation, while leveraging the strong foundation of economic and social linkages between our respective people, private sectors, and institutions. The excellent relations between India and the United States rest on the bedrock of kinship, commerce, and educational ties between the Indian and American people. Secretary Clinton and Minister Krishna affirmed the importance of expanding educational cooperation through exchanges and institutional collaboration and agreed on the need to expand the role of the private sector in strengthening this collaboration.

India is included in virtually all the educational exchange programs administered by the Bureau of Educational and Cultural Affairs (ECA) of the Department of State. In 2009, the ECA Bureau, which funds and administers the worldwide Fulbright Program through an annual appropriation from the U.S. Congress, provided a major increase in financial support for Fulbright academic exchanges with India. For the first time, the Government of India will partner with the U.S. to support and fund the program under a new joint Fulbright agreement.

The ECA Bureau's educational programs emphasize individual academic and leadership development, providing scholarships and exchange opportunities to U.S. students, scholars, teachers, and professionals for study, teaching, and research overseas, and to individuals from other countries to participate in educational exchange programs with the U.S. Programs are designed with merit-based selection processes, with the goal of meeting bilateral priorities and promoting access and inclusion. Sustaining interaction with and among the alumni of these programs is increasingly a priority for the Bureau as well. Virtually all these exchanges are administered in partnership with U.S. nongovernmental organizations through cooperative agreements awarded through the Bureau's congressionally mandated competitive grants process.

Since the 2001/02 academic year, India has sent the largest number of foreign students to the U.S. for university study of any country in the world. The State Department supports educational advising about U.S. higher education in India, sent a delegation of U.S. college and university presidents and senior U.S. government officials to India to promote U.S. higher education, hosted a delegation of Indian vice chancellors and university administrators to the United States, and cosponsored, with the U.S. Department of Commerce, the creation of a video and website to market U.S. higher education to Indian audiences.

The State Department values and encourages private, direct exchanges between U.S. and Indian institutions and counterparts, which supplement the government-sponsored exchanges that often serve as catalysts and can help to shape and support the role of all exchanges, both public and private, in serving the broad national interest. While a number of U.S. federal agencies support exchanges with India, the Department of State has the lead authority in negotiating formal exchange agreements and conducting international educational and exchange activities with other countries around the world, including India.

Fulbright Program

In September 1945, the freshman senator from Arkansas, J. William Fulbright, introduced a bill in the U.S. Congress that called for the use of proceeds from the sales of surplus war property to fund the "promotion of international good will through the exchange of students in the fields of education, culture and science." One year later, President Harry S. Truman signed the bill into law, and the young senator's vision of replacing swords with plowshares found its expression.

Today, Fulbright is the most widely recognized and prestigious international exchange program in the world, supported for more than half a century by the American people through an annual appropriation from the U.S. Congress and by the people of partner nations. The program—working with universities, schools, binational Fulbright commissions, government agencies, nongovernmental organizations, the private sector, and U.S. embassies abroad—actively seeks individuals of achievement and potential who represent the full diversity of their respective societies and selects nominees through open, merit-based competitions.

From its inception, the Fulbright Program has fostered bilateral relationships in which other countries and governments work with the U.S. to set joint priorities and shape the program to meet shared needs. The Fulbright Program is now the flagship international educational exchange program sponsored by the U.S. government, designed to increase mutual understanding between the people of the United States and the people of other countries. The Fulbright Program has provided approximately 294,000 participants—chosen for their academic merit and leadership potential—with the opportunity to study, teach and conduct research, exchange ideas, and contribute to finding solutions to shared international challenges.

On February 2, 1950, Indian Prime Minister and Minister of External Affairs Jawaharlal Nehru and U.S. Ambassador Loy W. Henderson signed the first Fulbright accord with India, establishing the Fulbright Foundation in India. In 2010, the U.S.-India Educational Foundation (USIEF), as the Fulbright Foundation is now called, will celebrate its 60th anniversary. Since its inception, the Fulbright Program with India has awarded approximately 8,200 Fulbright grants funded by the Department of State in almost every academic discipline. In addition, the USIEF has administered 8,700 other awards, including Fulbright-Hays Programs funded by the U.S. Department of Education and East-West Center awards, for a total of approximately 17,000 fellowships between the U.S. and India in the last 59 years.

On July 4, 2008, the United States Ambassador and the Indian Foreign Secretary signed an historic new Fulbright agreement, strengthening educational exchanges between the two countries. Under the new agreement, the Governments of India and the United States will implement the scholarship program as full partners awarding "Fulbright-Nehru" scholarships. The agreement also provides for expansion of the existing program with, for the first time, a direct financial contribution by the Government of India, and its co-chairing of the Board of Directors of the U.S.-India Educational Foundation, with the U.S. Ambassador and the Indian Foreign Secretary serving as the Honorary Chairs.

The Fulbright Program expands cooperation between the U.S. and India through the exchange of over 200 Indian and American Fulbright students, scholars, and teachers each year. In addition, ECA annually funds an additional 120 academic exchanges between the U.S. and India. The core program includes four major components:

- The **U.S. Student Program**, which sends about 49 American students to India annually;

- The **U.S. Scholar Program**, which sends approximately 20 lecturers and 20 researchers to India each year;

- The **Indian Student Program**, which brings to the U.S. 9 master's degree students (for up to two years), 15 PhD candidates for a year of dissertation-related research, and 8 Indian professionals for short-term specialized programs; and

- The **India Scholars Program**, which brings about 10 Indian lecturers and 27 Indian researchers each year to the U.S.

These programs are managed by the Bureau of Educational and Cultural Affairs in Washington and by the U.S.-India Educational Foundation in New Delhi. In the U.S., the Bureau is assisted by the Institute of International Education (IIE) in New York and its affiliate, the Council for International Exchange of Scholars (CIES), in Washington, D.C., in administering the student and scholar application, peer review, and nomination processes.

In India, students and scholars apply for awards directly to USIEF. USIEF organizes panels of Indian and American Fulbright alumni and government representatives, who review applications and nominate slates of candidates, who, once selected, are placed by CIES and IIE at U.S. academic institutions.

In 2006 the **Fulbright International Science and Technology Award** was created to attract outstanding foreign students worldwide to pursue doctoral degrees at leading U.S. research institutions in science and engineering fields. This highly competitive program was designed to be among the most prestigious international scholarships in science and technology and to demonstrate the United States' commitment to remain the premier destination for scientific study and research. Each year, approximately 40 students are selected. India first nominated participants in 2007 and has three Fulbright students in the U.S. on this program during the 2009/10 academic year.

Recent U.S. college graduates through advanced graduate students are eligible to apply through IIE for Fulbright scholarships. IIE convenes faculty panels to review applications and make recommendations to the Fulbright Foreign Scholarship Board, an independent, presidentially appointed board of distinguished private U.S. citizens that is responsible for the final selection of all Fulbright awardees.

This is the first year that the **Fulbright English Teaching Assistant (ETA) Program** has been active in India. The program places U.S. Fulbright Students as English teaching assistants in middle and high schools in the Delhi area. The program offers a structured framework for students to help teach English, act as mentors, gain knowledge of the host country and language, share their culture, and pursue individual research.

U.S. Fulbright scholars (postdoctoral/terminal degree holders) may apply for lecturing or research awards through the Council for International Exchange of Scholars, which annually convenes peer review panels that recommend candidates for awards. The peer review process is a central element of the Fulbright Program, serving as a guarantor of the program's scholarly integrity and nonpartisan, balanced, and nonpolitical character.

With the new Fulbright agreement in place, ECA and the U.S. Embassy in New Delhi will seek to further increase U.S.-India education cooperation by establishing a new **U.S.-India Higher Education Council**, a clearinghouse for the development of higher education institutional relations between the two countries. The council will create a framework to enhance information exchange and proactively support activities to facilitate higher education collaboration and research partnerships between universities in India and in the United States. A council director began work in fall 2009.

Tapping the talents of Fulbright scholars, USIEF holds over 60 academic or professional workshops annually, including several that include participants from across South Asia.

USIEF supports and facilitates alumni development and programming through its database for alumni and its work with Friends of Fulbright to India in the U.S. USIEF alumni have formed 18 Fulbright associations across India. Alumni associations support welcome events for new and returning Fulbrighters, advice sessions for Indian students interested in Fulbright and in U.S. education generally, USIEF anniversary celebrations, and mentoring for academics interested in developing their scholarly work.

The **Hubert H. Humphrey Fellowship Program**, a component of the Fulbright Program, brings to the U.S. outstanding mid-career professionals from countries in states of development or transition for one-year, nondegree programs that combine graduate-level academic work with substantive professional affiliations. The 2009–2010 cohort includes five Indian Humphrey Fellows studying in the areas of public policy analysis/public administration; agricultural and rural development; trafficking in persons; and educational administration, planning, and policy. The U.S.-India Educational Foundation in New Delhi is responsible for recruitment and nomination of candidates for the Humphrey Program. Nominated candidates are then reviewed in Washington, D.C., by panels of independent experts on India and the South and Central Asia region for recommendation to the Fulbright Foreign Scholarship Board. There are currently 129 Humphrey alumni from India.

Teacher Exchange

The **Fulbright Classroom Teacher Exchange Program** provides opportunities for U.S. and Indian teachers of math, science, and English to exchange teaching assignments and professional duties for a semester. Twelve teachers (six Indians and six Americans) will exchange positions in 2009/10.

IIE/AIFS Foundation Global Education Research Reports

INTERNATIONAL INDIA: A TURNING POINT IN EDUCATIONAL EXCHANGE WITH THE U.S.

25

The **Distinguished Fulbright Awards in Teaching Program** provides opportunities for highly accomplished teachers from the U.S. and selected countries abroad to pursue individual projects, conduct research, take courses for professional development, and lead master classes or seminars for teachers and students. International teachers are hosted at Vanderbilt University. Two teachers from India will participate in 2009/10.

The **Teaching Excellence and Achievement (TEA) Program** brings English as a Foreign Language and social science teachers from around the world to the U.S. for a six-week professional development program including coursework, curriculum development, and a three-week internship in a U.S. school. In 2008, 11 Indian teachers participated in the program, and five U.S. teachers made reciprocal visits to India. The next cohort of 11 Indian teachers will begin the TEA program in September 2009.

Under the **India Summer Teachers' Project,** eight American secondary teachers of math, science, and English traveled to India in July 2009 where they taught and collaborated with Indian teachers and students for five weeks.

The **International Leaders in Education Program (ILEP)** provides teachers from the Near East, South Asia, East Asia and Pacific, and the Western Hemisphere with opportunities to develop expertise in their subject areas, enhance their teaching skills, and increase their knowledge about the United States. During the semester-long program, teachers audit university coursework at the graduate level and participate in eight-week internships at local schools. The program continues to support the teachers' collaboration with U.S. schools through alumni grants. Eight teachers from India participated in the 2008/09 programs.

Study Abroad

The **Benjamin A. Gilman International Scholarship Program** provides scholarships to U.S. undergraduates with financial need for study abroad, including students from diverse backgrounds and students going to nontraditional study abroad destinations. Established under the International Academic Opportunity Act of 2000, Gilman Scholarships provide up to $5,000 for American students to pursue overseas study for college credit. Students of critical need languages are eligible for up to $3,000 in additional funding as part of the Gilman Critical Need Language Supplement program. In 2008/09, 38 Gilman scholars studied in India, including one Gilman Critical Need Language Supplement award recipient in spring 2009.

Study of Indic Languages

The United States Government has designated a number of Indic languages for inclusion in a national effort to increase Americans' knowledge and mastery of critical languages. The State Department supports language-related exchanges of teachers and high school, undergraduate, and graduate students as part of this effort. The **Critical Language Scholarship (CLS) Program for Intensive Summer Institutes** provides fully funded, group-based intensive language instruction and cultural enrichment experiences at the beginning, intermediate, and advanced levels of Bengali, Hindi, Punjabi, and Urdu. U.S. citizen undergraduate, graduate, and doctoral students study these languages in India for seven to ten weeks under the CLS Program. Fifty-seven U.S. undergraduate and graduate students spent ten weeks in 2009 studying Indic languages in Kolkata (Bengali), Raipur (Hindi), Chandigarh (Punjabi), and Lucknow (Urdu) under the **Critical Language Scholarships for Intensive Summer Institutes.**

In addition, **Critical Language Enhancement Awards** are awarded to Fulbright U.S. student grantees for study of Bengali, Gujarati, Hindi, Marathi, Punjabi, and Urdu to augment their language skills to carry out research projects before and throughout their grant period in India. In 2009, there were nine CLEA Fulbright awardees in India.

The **Fulbright Foreign Language Teaching Assistant (FLTA) Program** provides young college teachers of English, or those training to be teachers of English in other countries, an opportunity to refine their teaching skills, increase their English language proficiency, and extend their knowledge of the United States while strengthening the instruction of foreign languages at U.S. colleges and universities. Applicants must be between 21 and 29 years old when they apply. Selected FLTA fellows from India will teach Bengali, Gujarati, Hindi, and Urdu at selected U.S. campuses during their nine-month grants. Thirteen FLTAs from India are on U.S. campuses during the 2009/10 academic year.

Undergraduate Programs

The **Near East and South Asia Undergraduate Exchange Program (NESA UGRAD)** provides scholarships for one academic year of nondegree study at a U.S. college or university. The program provides a substantive exchange experience to a diverse group of emerging student leaders from underrepresented groups in the Middle East, North Africa, and South Asia, including India, Bangladesh, Pakistan, and Nepal. In 2009/10, the program will provide one academic year of study to five Indian undergraduate students.

Research Centers

The **American Institute of Indian Studies (AIIS)** receives support from ECA through the Council of American Overseas Research Centers (CAORC). AIIS was founded in 1961 to increase and improve understanding between India and the United States through academic research into various aspects of Indian life and thought. The Institute is headquartered at Gurgaon just outside New Delhi and maintains branches in Calcutta, Chennai, and Pune. AIIS fellows represent all fields in the humanities and social sciences and some fields in the sciences. AIIS provides services to any U.S. scholar conducting research in India. AIIS also secures research approvals and visas, offers accommodation at its guest houses, arranges access to archives, and provides services that permit scholars to focus on their work. In 2007/08 AIIS supported 41 scholars in India. In 2008/09 AIIS supported 37 scholars in India. AIIS also provides language instruction for ECA Critical Language Scholarship and Critical Language Enhancement Award grantees.

English Programs

English Language Programs have gained importance among the ECA Bureau's programs with India and other countries, reflecting growing awareness of the role of English in opening doors to educational and economic opportunity as well as to study in the U.S. Around the world, English study is in high demand by governments as well as students and their families. Providing English training to talented Indian students from disadvantaged sectors, who would not otherwise have the opportunity to learn English well, removes a critical barrier that allows them to compete to take part in exchanges and study in the United States, helping to make exchanges more fully representative of Indian society.

A State Department **Regional English Language Officer (RELO)** is based at the U.S. Embassy in New Delhi. The RELO organizes and participates in teacher training seminars and workshops, advises embassies in the region on issues related to English teaching, conducts needs assessments, and offers guidance on all aspects of an academic program. ECA's Office of English Language Programs is establishing a second RELO position in India and expects to have that RELO in place in 2010.

Created in 2004 as a program for countries in the Middle East and South Asia, the **English Access Microscholarship Program** has now expanded to over 50 countries worldwide. The program provides a foundation of English language skills to bright 14- to 18-year-olds from disadvantaged sectors through after-school classes and intensive summer learning activities. In 2008/09, 1,000 students in six locations in India participated in the program. The Access Program provides students with an opportunity to study English, increasing their ability to participate in the socioeconomic development of their country and to gain an appreciation for American culture and values.

The **E-Teacher Scholarship Program** seeks to improve the quality of overseas English language teaching through the use of innovative distance learning technology. Participants are English teaching professionals who receive instruction from U.S. experts in current English language teaching methods and techniques. Courses in the program include Assessment, English for Business, and English for Law, Teaching

Critical Thinking, and Teaching English to Young Learners. In the 2009/10 school year, the seven courses offered include: Critical Thinking in the EFL (English as a Foreign Language) Curriculum, Teaching English to Young Learners, Building Teaching Skills through the Interactive Web, English for Specific Purposes Best Practices, English as a Foreign Language Assessment, Methods Course I: Survey of Best Practices in TESOL, and Methods Course II: Developing EFL Literacy through Project-Based Learning. In 2008/09, nine teachers from India participated in the online graduate level teacher training.

The **English Language Specialist Program** recruits U.S. academics in the fields of TEFL/TESL and applied linguistics for short-term (two- to four-week) assignments. In 2008/09, four English Language Specialists visited India to work on assignments at the request of the U.S. Embassy in New Delhi.

The **English Language Fellow Program** sends highly qualified U.S. educators in the field of teaching English to speakers of other languages on ten-month fellowships to academic institutions in India. Fellows work with local faculty at the university to build English language teaching capacity. In 2009/10, three senior English Language Fellows have been placed in India to present workshops and seminars to teachers of English on a variety of topics, including English language teaching methodology, critical thinking, and U.S. studies.

The Office of English Language Programs also produces the *English Teaching Forum*, a quarterly professional journal for overseas teachers of English that focuses on teaching methods and classroom practices. India is receiving 2,000 copies of the U.S. Department of State publication this year.

Educational Advising

EducationUSA Advising is available at seven EducationUSA Advising Centers in India at Fulbright Commission offices in Chennai, Kolkata, Mumbai, and New Delhi, and at satellite centers in Ahmedabad, Bengaluru, Hyderabad, and Manipal. USIEF also has a "help desk" in Dibrugarh. These centers reach out to more than 500,000 students annually. An ECA-supported Regional Educational Advising Coordinator for India is based in Mumbai.

According to *Open Doors: Report on International Educational Exchange*, published annually by IIE with support from the ECA Bureau, India has been the number one sending place of origin since 2001/02, when it surpassed China. In academic year 2008/09, there were 103,260 students from India studying in the United States (up 9.2 percent from the previous year). The 2000/01 academic year marked a new surge in enrollments from India, with an increase of 30 percent followed by two more years of double-digit growth (22 percent in 2002/03 and 12 percent in 2003/04).

U.S. Studies

The **Study of the United States Institutes for Global Student Leaders** are intensive academic programs whose purpose is to provide undergraduate student leaders with a deeper understanding of the United States, while at the same time enhancing their leadership skills. The Institutes include four components: an academic residency component that focuses on the role and influence of principles and values in American society, such as democracy, the rule of law, individual rights, freedom of expression, equality, and tolerance; a leadership development training component; community service; and an educational travel tour. In 2009, 19 Indian students will participate.

Study of the United States Institutes for Scholars are designed to strengthen curricula and improve the quality of teaching about the United States overseas. These Institutes host multinational groups of university faculty or secondary school educators. Each Institute is thematically focused on a field or topic of U.S. studies. Participants interact with American scholars, meet with experts in their disciplines, visit civic institutions, and explore the diversity and culture of the United States. In 2009, eight Indian scholars will participate.

Conclusion

Educational exchange programs, while benefiting individuals by increasing their knowledge and enabling them to build personal and professional relationships in the country of their exchange, also serve broader interests, by strengthening mutual understanding between peoples and among nations. The effectiveness of these programs is evident in its many alumni, who hold positions of leadership across all sectors and throughout the institutions of both societies, thereby building a foundation of trust and collaboration between the U.S. and India.

Background on the Bureau of Educational and Cultural Affairs
The Department of State is the Executive Branch Department authorized by the Congress of the United States to conduct official U.S. public diplomacy programs abroad, including educational exchanges. Exchange programs reflect the long-term foreign policy interests of the U.S. in promoting increased understanding and constructive interaction between individuals, institutions, and publics in the United States and other countries. The State Department's Bureau of Educational and Cultural Affairs (ECA) supports a wide range of educational, professional, and cultural exchanges involving educators, students, scientists, artists, government officials, journalists, NGO representatives, and members of the business community, among others. The purpose of these exchanges is to increase mutual understanding between the people of the United States and the people of other countries, as embodied in the Fulbright-Hays legislation (Mutual Educational and Cultural Affairs Exchange Act of 1961.) The Bureau supports academic exchanges on a bilateral basis, through the Public Affairs Section of U.S. embassies and binational Fulbright Commissions, in cooperation with partner governments in more than 150 countries.

Chapter Three

INDIAN GOVERNMENTAL AND POLICY INITIATIVES FOR U.S.-INDIA EDUCATIONAL EXCHANGE

SAM PITRODA, ADVISOR TO THE PRIME MINISTER OF INDIA ON PUBLIC INFORMATION INFRASTRUCTURE AND INNOVATIONS

The National Knowledge Commission (NKC) was a visionary endeavor born out of the belief of Dr. Manmohan Singh, the Prime Minister of India, that the 21st century would belong to knowledge. While industrial production dominated the economies of the past, the new competitive economies of the future will be driven by knowledge. With this premise in mind, the NKC embarked on the task of creating a blueprint to revamp the country's knowledge institutions and infrastructure to meet the challenges of the knowledge century. Building a vibrant and innovative education system is crucial in a country such as India, which must address the daunting challenges posed by demography, disparity, and development. With its unique demographic dividend, India has an unprecedented opportunity to play a major role in the global economy and in the welfare and development of societies worldwide.

To achieve a holistic perspective on knowledge, the commission focused its attention on five core areas of the knowledge paradigm: **access to knowledge, knowledge concepts, creation of knowledge, knowledge applications,** and **delivery of services.** During its three-year term, NKC reached out to numerous stakeholders and submitted around 300 recommendations in a variety of areas such as right to education, languages, translation, libraries, national knowledge network, portals, health information network, school education, higher education, more students in mathematics and science, legal education, medical education, management education, engineering education, more quality PhDs, open and distance education, open education resources, intellectual property rights, legal framework for public-funded research, national science and social science foundations, innovation, entrepreneurship, vocational education and training (VET), traditional health systems, agriculture, enhancing quality of life, and e-governance.

NKC's policy recommendations on education have focused on the need for generational changes in primary, secondary, vocational, higher, and professional education. Access to primary and secondary education remains a tremendous challenge in India. Out of the 200 million children in the 6–14 age group, around 30 million

IIE/AIFS Foundation Global Education Research Reports
INTERNATIONAL INDIA: A TURNING POINT IN EDUCATIONAL EXCHANGE WITH THE U.S.

33

never enroll in school, and 85 million drop out. To create a strong foundation for a knowledge society, these marginalized children have to be included in the system. In order to transform a nation into a knowledge society capable of competing in the global market, a focused agenda for skill development is imperative. Today, there is a significant gap between what the education system is producing and the skill requirements of the marketplace. With 57 percent of the country's youth suffering from unemployability, lack of vocational skills is a critical problem in India. To harness our demographic dividend and to strengthen the link between education and employability, we need to overhaul the system of vocational education and training in the country. The higher education system is also in crisis. Our gross enrollment ratio (GER) for higher education (the percentage of the 18–24 age group enrolled in a higher education institution) is 10 percent, which is far below the average GER of 25 percent in developed countries. With 55 million residents below the age of 25 and an abysmally low number of high-quality universities, India is likely to see the supply of education—especially higher education—outstripped by demand in the coming years. This considerable shortage will have to be addressed if we are to develop our human capital. Further, a strong "ecosystem" of research is a crucial component of a vibrant knowledge- and skills-based economy, but India's performance in this area has been sub par. In 2002, the number of researchers per million inhabitants of the United States was 4,373; the figure for Japan was 5,084; Germany had 3,208; and even China had 633 researchers per million inhabitants—while India had only 112.

At NKC, we have submitted detailed recommendations on how to address these challenges through policy interventions at the level of the central government. We have recommended enacting central legislation affirming the right to education, with the goal of enhancing access to primary education as well as promoting qualitative improvements in the school system, including curriculum reform. The Right to Education Bill has now been passed by the government and will be a crucial first step towards addressing concerns of access. We have suggested reforms in the higher education system to address the three challenges of expansion, excellence, and equity and have recommended greater flexibility in vocational education and training, along with more innovative delivery models. We have also suggested reforms to improve the quality of original research in the country and measures for enriching the synergies between teaching and research.

However, the magnitude of the task in front of us requires not just local initiatives but also a push to explore educational collaboration on a global scale. Increased global flows of people, services, and technology are increasingly rendering borders irrelevant, and we need to tap into the advantages provided by this mobility. To create a competitive knowledge economy, India needs to build innovative and sustainable partnerships with other countries, especially the U.S., which was the powerhouse of new ideas in the 20th century. With India sending around 100,000 students to study in the U.S. every year, more than any other country, the need for a more equitable platform for the exchange of ideas and knowledge becomes even more pertinent. Further, the new government in India is focused on heralding a "decade of innovation" to foster the next generation of knowledge creation and management systems in India. One aspect of this decade will have to involve looking beyond our national borders for mutually beneficial collaborations and solutions.

U.S. expertise in the education sector would be useful for India at many levels. Innovative American ideas could be tapped for recruiting talent into teaching (for example, Teach for America now has an Indian variant, Teach for India), modernizing curricula, improving the accreditation framework in higher education, enhancing research efforts in core areas, managing public-private partnerships in the education sector, and using technology for education delivery. For India, the critical lessons would involve embracing the flexible, highly decentralized, and multifaceted U.S. education system as best it can and moving away from a centrist, didactic approach to education that currently prevails in India. For the U.S., one catalyst for deeper engagement with India could be learning from its educational successes in the fields of information and communication technologies, engineering, technology, mathematics, and science. Further, India could provide a challenging platform for research institutes and U.S. students to experiment with new models for innovation at the "bottom of the pyramid." For American students, exposure to Indian culture would be a great way to challenge ethnocentric viewpoints and prepare for an increasingly multiethnic, global work culture.

Technology will play a key role in realizing this collaboration. At NKC we have emphasized the role of information and communication technologies (ICT) in improving the delivery of education. Our recommendation to create an electronic digital broadband network with adequate capabilities to interconnect all our knowledge institutions throughout the country has been accepted by the government, and implementation is currently underway. This National Knowledge Network will eventually connect 5,000 nodes in the country and bring about unprecedented sharing of resources. While the network is presently envisioned as a national one, eventually we hope to reap more benefits through cross-border collaborations, especially with the United States. Open and distance learning in higher education and virtual connections between research institutions in the two countries can open up tremendous opportunities for a two-way exchange of ideas. India can leverage content and delivery models for open and distance learning that have been developed in recognized American institutions such as MIT and University of Phoenix Online. The U.S. can play a pioneering role in bringing innovative delivery models that address concerns of access to Indian secondary and postsecondary institutions. We have to prepare ourselves for the next leap in education. The new model of education will not be about "chalk and blackboards" but will challenge time and space constraints in global, virtual classrooms. New technology-enabled delivery systems will provide opportunities for the next generation of learners from the two countries to collaborate on an equal footing.

A vast array of collaborative initiatives could be explored in secondary and higher education. Successful examples from the U.S. school system, such as charter schools and the Bank Street School initiative, can be contextualized and adapted in India with

America's help. Liberalization of the higher education sector will remain critical to meeting the gap between demand and supply by allowing private players and foreign institutions to enter the country. To this end, the government is debating the Foreign Educational Institutions (Regulation of Entry and Operations, Maintenance of Quality and Prevention of Commercialization) Bill. The aim of the bill is to ease entry of reputable foreign education providers while providing a level playing field. This would be a tremendous opportunity for U.S. institutions waiting to explore the higher education landscape in India. However, mechanisms would need to be in place to ensure that the quality of the institutes coming into India is not compromised. As India prepares to reform and upgrade its education sector to support its development goals and respond to the challenges of the 21st century, it should look at innovative models to establish world-class universities, research laboratories, and centers of excellence, including tapping the expertise and resources of foreign universities. Collaboration in the field of higher education will be critical to the next phase of engagement between India and the United States.

Further, new Indian higher education institutions could conduct research and PhD programs with leading U.S. institutions and organizations like MIT, Lincoln Labs, Bell Labs, Johns Hopkins University, and Carnegie Mellon University, and could become focal points of excellence in high technology. The intellectual capital developed and exchange of talent and ideas would benefit both countries. Mechanisms could also be devised for structured and frequent exchange of talented teachers between Indian and American universities. Synergies could also be explored in intellectual property rights, agriculture, and health education. Also, incentives must be created for more Americans to study abroad in India (India is currently number 17 on the list of destinations for Americans studying abroad), which will lead to a richer understanding of Indian culture in the U.S. and deepen people-to-people exchange. To achieve this, customizing the program with the help of enthusiastic local partners will be critical in order to create an environment suitable for foreign students.

However, it is not just the elementary, secondary, and higher education sectors that need new models of collaboration but also the vocational education stream. The U.S. community college model could provide flexible models that could be adaptable to the Indian vocational education and training sector. U.S. and Indian companies could also work together to solve the skills gap in the country by jointly sponsoring selected industrial training institutes (ITIs) in India, or perhaps through setting up new institutes.

These linkages between the two countries could create the necessary platform for long-term synergies in the education sector, the productive effects of which will spill over to many more interlinked areas. For decades, the U.S.-India relationship in the knowledge economy has been predicated on the premise of brain drain, which sees India suffering the loss of local capacity in fields critical to development. To emerge as a key player in the global knowledge economy, India needs to foster a new outlook of "brain gain" that will not only benefit it but also prove to be equally beneficial for the United States. Exercising this form of soft power will not only strengthen ties and lead to better mutual understanding but also lay the groundwork for a more engaged diplomatic relationship between the two countries.

Chapter Four

Internationalization of Indian Higher Education

Pawan Agarwal, Senior Indian Civil Servant and Visiting Scholar,
Indian Council for International Economic Research, New Delhi

Internationalization is an idea that originally referred to helping students develop international understanding and intercultural skills with the goal of preparing students to be active in a globalizing world. Now, its definition has broadened to include cross-border institutions and programs that contribute to mobility of students and faculty (De Wit, 2008).

Although Indian universities have been hosting foreign students and scholars on their campuses for many years, "internationalization" of higher education has not been discussed specifically in India until recently. In the year 2000, the planning document of the University Grants Commission (UGC) noted that "in the context of globalization of higher education, it is necessary to evolve a policy to promote the free flow of students from other nations to India as well as allow Indian students to get educated in other countries."

In recent years, concern about growing numbers of Indians studying abroad and the country's inability to attract foreign students has grown. Permitting foreign institutions to operate in India is fiercely debated. Several Indian institutions have ventured abroad. All these developments suggest that the issue of internationalization is growing in importance for Indian higher education.

This chapter examines the current status of internationalization of Indian higher education. The chapter begins with an overview of India's growing global influence and current status of its higher education. It then examines patterns and trends in outward and inward student mobility and finally looks at the status of foreign provision in India and related policy debates.

Higher Education and India's Growing Global Influence

India is the world's second most-populous country, and its population will overtake that of China by 2028. Over the next 25 years, India's population is projected to rise by almost 350 million, twice as fast as the U.S., Western Europe, and China combined. The youth population (15- to 24-year-olds) is expected to rise even faster (United Nations, 2008).

India is in the midst of a middle-class boom. By 2025, 100 million young people—twice the number of all young people in North America and 25 percent more than in all of Europe—will come from middle-class Indian backgrounds and have a global outlook, rising aspirations, and good incomes (Shukla, Dwivedi, & Sharma, 2004). A large proportion of this group is likely to scout globally for the best higher education options. The Indian diaspora is the world's third-largest, after the British and Chinese diasporas, with significant numbers of people of Indian origin living in over 70 countries, including many advanced countries, and the existence of this overseas network will contribute to internationalization trends in Indian higher education.

At comparable prices, India is already the world's fourth-largest economy and, with its consistent healthy growth despite global economic recession, it is likely to become a global economic powerhouse. Over the past decade, the Indian economy has undergone a structural transformation from a largely rural, agrarian economy to an urban economy based on manufacturing and services. As a result, demand for skilled labor adapted to this new economy is on the rise.

Factors that have contributed to India's growing global clout include favorable demography, rapid economic growth coupled with rising prosperity, and a large and growing diaspora population. "India's global brand image has moved from a poor impoverished nation combined with outdated socialist ideas and a Victorian bureaucracy, to one of a tech-savvy, globalized twenty-first century intellectual power" (Gupta, 2006).

Interest in Indian higher education is on the rise as well. Indian higher education has three natural advantages: relative comfort with the English language, a historically strong and well-regarded system (though this is fast eroding), and low cost of living. Considering these advantages, India has the potential to become one of the world's major higher education destinations. However, India needs to get its policies and institutions right if it aspires to become a major global player.

Several endemic and structural problems plague the country's higher education system. Although India's total national higher education enrollment is the world's third-largest at around 12.8 million (surpassed only by China and the U.S.), the country lags behind in relative terms, accommodating just 11 percent of eligible people. Female participation rates are even lower. The bulk of this enrollment is in university-affiliated colleges that often follow outdated curricula.

The total number of universities and colleges in India is very large (about 22,500—almost the same number as the rest of world combined); but with an average of just 600 students in each, many of them are unviable (Agarwal, 2009). The system is highly fragmented and riddled with contradictions.

A majority of the country's students (88.9 percent) are enrolled in undergraduate programs, with merely 9.4 percent enrolled in postgraduate and just 0.7 percent in doctoral programs. Enrollment by major field of study is skewed in favor of the arts and humanities (45 percent), followed by science (20.5 percent) and commerce (18 percent). Only 17 percent of students pursue professional studies, which are dominated by engineering and medicine (Agarwal, 2009). Given this distribution of fields of study, a large part of higher education lacks vocational focus and churns out graduates who have difficulty securing employment.

Vocational education and training that cater to entry-level skills are small and separated from higher education. They have low prestige and poor quality; hence, demand for vocational programs is meager despite a huge shortage of people with vocational skills. Training needs for high-end vocational skills, particularly in the area of information technology, are met by the burgeoning private education sector. In certain fields like engineering, medicine, management, nursing, and teaching, private institutions account for more than four-fifths of all enrollments. With ineffective accreditation and regulatory loopholes in the private education sector, perverse incentives often dominate, and quality suffers as a result.

Although government funding has gone up over the past couple of years, public funds continue to be scarce and unevenly distributed. As a result, most institutions face financial hardships and have raised fees, particularly for professional programs, to substitute or supplement public funds. This has made higher education expensive—since only a small number of students qualify for loans, access to higher education is restricted.

With a growing number of young people and rising prosperity, demand for higher education is destined to grow. Along with increasing demand, students and their families are also increasingly willing to pay. Consequently, the private sector has grown dramatically in recent years, but significant unmet demand remains. To fill this gap, foreign institutions are eager to take advantage of opportunities in the Indian market, and a large and growing numbers of students leave the country for their studies.

Outward Mobility

The number of Indians who leave the country to study has increased over the years. No longer confined to the rich or the intellectual elite, studying abroad is now a possibility even for ordinary students from middle-income families. In just over 40 years there has been a 24-fold increase in the number of Indian students abroad, from 11,192 in 1965 to 268,000 in 2008. Though this is less than in China, where the numbers sharply grew from a few thousand in the 1960s to 417,350 in 2008, it is more than twice the global growth rate—the total number of internationally mobile students grew from 290,000 in 1963 to 2.9 million today. Currently, Indians constitute about 7.5 percent of the world's mobile students, the second-largest group of students from a single country (after China).

About a decade ago, the main destination for Indians seeking foreign degrees was the U.S., with some going to the UK. Though the U.S. continues to lead as the most favored destination, it is less predominant now. In 2000, three-fourths of Indian students went to the U.S.; this was reduced to about half in 2008. Now Indians study in a more diverse set of countries, with countries like Australia and the UK serving as important destinations because of their large Indian diaspora communities, which tend to attract a large number of Indian students. Table 4.1 gives growth trends by country in outward mobility and current stock of Indian diaspora in destination countries.

TABLE 4.1: TRENDS IN OUTWARD MOBILITY FROM INDIA

Country	Indian Diaspora	Number of Students		Increase (%)
		2000	2008	
U.S.	2,662,112	47,411	94,563	200
Australia	235,000	6,195	96,555	1,558
UK	1,600,000	4,649	35,245	758
China	...	...	7,234	...
Canada	960,000	1,431	7,200	503
Singapore	320,000	...	6,700	...
Germany	35,000	1,412	5,200	378
Malaysia	2,400,000	714	2,600	364
New Zealand	105,000	355	2,500	704
Sweden	11,000	92	1,500	1,630
France	75,000	239	640	268
Japan	20,589	...	544	...
Switzerland	13,500	84	400	476
Other countries	...	1,000	5,000	...
Total	23,000,000	63,000	267,889	425

Note: Countries are ranked in the order of the number of Indian higher education students studying in each country in 2008.

Source: Compiled by the author from OECD Database, UNESCO Institute of Statistics Database, EUROSTAT Database and in some cases from country-based sources: the U.S. (Bhandari & Chow, 2008), Australia (AEI), Atlas of International Student Mobility, and Indian diaspora data from Ministry of Overseas Indian Affairs (updated where current data from source country available)

The numbers for 2008 in the above table may be somewhat overstated, since significant enrollment figures for the Australian vocational education and training (VET) and English language intensive courses for overseas students (ELICOS) sectors are included. Counting higher education enrollment alone for Australia (27,455 out of 96,555), the total number of Indian students abroad would be almost 199,000 in 2008, which still represents a more than threefold increase over 2000 numbers.

There are several reasons for this remarkable increase over the past few years. The actual number of Indian students in Australia has grown dramatically. There has also been a change in the way international students are counted in the UK, resulting in a 25 percent upward revision of the number of Indian students studying there. This, along with a robust growth over the previous year, has raised the numbers for the UK (Lightfoot, 2009). Between 2006/07 and 2007/08 there was a 12.8 percent increase in the number of Indian students in the U.S. (Bhandari & Chow, 2008). Thus, these three main destination countries experienced a spectacular growth in Indian students, hosting almost 85 percent of all Indian students abroad. Indian students make up the largest group of overseas students in the U.S., which is the top destination country for Indian students. They also form the second-largest group of overseas students in the UK and Australia.

In recent years, Asian neighbors including China, Singapore, and Malaysia have begun to attract significant numbers of Indian students. These three countries host more than 6 percent of Indian students abroad. If the significant numbers of students studying in United Arab Emirates, Qatar, and Nepal (where an Indian private institution has set up a campus) are included, it would go up even higher. Indian students are now going to all of the world's important destination countries in increasing numbers, with the most significant growth occurring in New Zealand, Sweden, Cyprus, and Ireland. Two important traditional destinations, Canada and Germany, also continue to attract a large number of Indian students. All countries that plan to enter the increasingly competitive international student market see India as an extremely lucrative market and have begun to make inroads.

While China continues to send the largest number of students abroad, more than twice as many as from India, recent trends suggest that the gap between China and India is closing. With a declining youth population and a dramatic increase in domestic higher education provision (a 2.5 million-student increase, which amounts to adding one new UK higher education system every year), the number of Chinese students accessing an overseas education is likely to decline over time. In comparison, outward mobility from India may not increase as rapidly as at present, but because of the rising population of young people and limited growth in domestic capacity, a large number of Indian students will continue to study abroad for at least the next two decades. With an estimated 1.5 percent growth rate in outbound mobility for China and 6 percent for India, India is on track to surpass China as the main source country of international students by 2025.

Several factors will impact outward mobility from India. While growth will continue overall, especially for emerging nations and new destinations, there will also be a slowdown in outward mobility to the U.S., the UK, and Australia. The coming years will see more aggressive marketing by all host nations targeting the rapidly growing Indian market. While many advanced nations will take advantage of the limited capacity of the graduate education and research sector in India, countries such as Australia, with its well-developed vocational education sector, will likely target India's weakness in this area.

The implications of a growing number of Indians studying abroad have already been a matter of public debate for decades. Is the country losing precious capital as students stock up on foreign currency to pay for tuition and living expenses abroad?

Would an increase in domestic capacity help in reducing outward mobility? Often the debate is represented in simplistic terms. A close look, however, shows that the estimates for revenue loss are grossly inflated and more than offset by the growing inbound remittances usually associated with increased outward mobility. The notion of brain drain is also being replaced by new developments termed brain gain, brain circulation, and even reverse brain drain.

Thus, concerns about revenue loss and brain drain are misplaced. Contrary to the common belief that building domestic capacity would enable the country to retain students, it is now thought that student migration is strongly affected by the promise of wage opportunities, not constraints in the domestic educational capacity of the source countries (Rosenzweig, 2006).

For countries like India, outward mobility may be beneficial. The focus of public policy has therefore shifted from preventing brain drain to managing migration better by promoting the integration of the migrants in host societies. A well-managed migration, where student flows play an important role, could contribute to increased employment and rapid economic growth both for India and globally. Migrant workers could become the nucleus of a worldwide network harnessed for the home country's development. Such networks could enable knowledge transfer and promote new businesses in the home country.

Inward Mobility

Although ancient Indian universities are known to have hosted foreign students and scholars from around the world, modern Indian universities have primarily focused on domestic students and have traditionally looked inward. A few universities have received foreign students but purely out of altruism. The Indian government treats inviting foreign students, particularly from friendly, neighboring countries, as a part of public diplomacy (Agarwal, 2008b).

International students have traditionally come from neighboring countries in South Asia and countries that have large Indian diaspora communities. The Association of Indian Universities (AIU), the agency that collects mobility statistics, faces many difficulties in collecting and collating data, particularly for students from neighboring countries— Nepal, Bhutan, and Bangladesh—whose borders with India are porous. Thus, there are many gaps in data on international students in India, though data are available from 1988/89 onward. Long-term trends based on AIU data show that the numbers stood at 11,844 in 1988/89, steadily increasing during the first half of the 1990s to a peak of over 13,707 students in 1993/94, and declining steadily thereafter. A marked drop occurred in 1996/97, and by the end of the millennium the number of international students in India had halved. While many developed countries, especially the UK and Australia, were aggressively marketing their education abroad, India stood inactive. However, the numbers began to grow from 2001/02 onwards, after India adopted a more positive approach, streamlining the visa regime, and allowing universities and colleges to admit 15 percent more international students than allowed by their sanctioned intake. Currently, India hosts 18,594 international students (AIU, 2009).

International students in India come from about 195 countries; 28 of them send more than 100 students. Iran sends the highest number, followed by United Arab Emirates, Nepal, Ethiopia, Saudi Arabia, and Kenya. Over 90 percent of students come from the developing countries of Asia and Africa, with two-thirds coming from Asia and one-fourth from Africa. Nearly half of the students come from what might be considered low-income countries and one-fourth from the upper-middle income countries (AIU, 2007).

In terms of regional distribution, South and Central Asia lead with more than 30 percent. About 20 percent of students are from North Africa and the Middle East. Trends over the past 18 years (table 4.2) indicate that, while in earlier years countries in North Africa and Sub-Saharan Africa (Kenya, Sudan, Ethiopia, Nigeria, Kenya, and Somalia) sent the largest numbers, by the late 1990s numbers from these countries (except Ethiopia) had fallen dramatically. Southeast Asia (Malaysia, Thailand, and Vietnam) had previously sent a significant number of students, but those numbers have since fallen (AIU, 2000, 2007, 2009). Mauritius, with its sizeable Indian diaspora, still sends about 400 students. In recent years, most international students in India have come from the Middle East (Iran, UAE, Saudi Arabia, Oman, and Yemen).

TABLE 4.2: COUNTRIES SENDING THE MOST INTERNATIONAL STUDENTS TO INDIA (1988/89 TO 2006/07)

	1988/89	1998/99	2006/07
1	Kenya (2,332)	Kenya (639)	Iran (2,180)
2	Sudan (1,692)	Nepal (574)	UAE (1,878)
3	Jordan (1,247)	Bangladesh (461)	Nepal (1,728)
4	Nepal (912)	Ethiopia (403)	Ethiopia (1,033)
5	Malaysia (824)	Sri Lanka (368)	Saudi Arabia (771)
6	Iran (553)	Sudan (245)	Kenya (621)
7	Ethiopia (455)	Thailand (197)	U.S. (615)
8	Sri Lanka (430)	Uganda (196)	Oman (608)
9	Somalia (429)	Iran (108)	Yemen (598)
10	Nigeria (339)	Vietnam (88)	Bhutan (531)
11	Bangladesh (252)	Jordan (60)	Sri Lanka (466)
12	Thailand (187)	Afghanistan (59)	Korea (452)

Source: Association of Indian Universities, 2000, 2007, 2009.

India's neighbors send a much larger number of students to advanced countries than to India. For instance, in 2006/07 Nepal sent 8,936 students to the U.S., compared to merely 1,728 to India. Similarly, Pakistan, Sri Lanka, and Bangladesh sent 5,345; 2,591; and 2,305 students to the U.S., respectively, compared to merely 7; 466; and 361 students to India (Agarwal, 2008a).

Most students coming to India from advanced nations pursue short-term study abroad programs. Though the overall number of foreign students is still small, it has been growing in recent years. For instance, according to *Open Doors* data, the number of U.S. students in India increased from 382 in 1993/94 to 3,146 in 2007/08. While this increase is encouraging, the absolute numbers are small especially when compared with the number of Indian students who study in the U.S. (103,260 in 2008/09). The small number is particularly striking in comparison to the number of U.S. students who studied in other "nontraditional" study abroad destinations such as China (11,064) or even Costa Rica (5,383) (Bhandari & Chow, 2008).

The majority of international students in India, 77.6 percent, are enrolled at the undergraduate level, 12.5 percent are enrolled in postgraduate studies, and only 1.4 percent of students are in research programs. International students are mainly concentrated in the western (especially Maharashtra) and southern parts of India. They prefer to study in and around large cities including Delhi, Mumbai, Chennai, and Pune. The top 10 Indian host universities account for 80 percent of the total number of students. At the very top is Indira Gandhi National Open University, enrolling 3,925 students in its programs. However, the figures may be overstated to the extent that many of these students are enrolled in distance education programs and are not physically in India.

The top 10 host institutions include four private universities—Symbiosis International University (3,554), Manipal University (1,325), Bharati Vidyapeeth (473), and Jamia Hamdard (349). Both admissions and fees are tightly regulated by the government for private institutions. To encourage international student enrollments, private institutions have been allowed 15 percent supernumerary seats to admit foreign students and enjoy greater leeway in deciding the fees for foreign students. As a result, private institutions are playing an increasingly important role in attracting international students.

Despite the upward trend, the growth of international students in India is strikingly low compared to that in China. China, which hosted only a few hundred students in the early 1990s, now hosts about 200,000 students, while in India this number increased from about 13,000 students in 1990/91 to the current 18,594. There are several reasons for this. Academic structure, academic calendars, grading procedures, and methods of instruction in Indian higher education need to change and align with global norms to ensure that more international students enroll. For example, international students from certain countries are used to being able to select their courses, while Indian students generally take sequenced courses, mostly within their discipline of study. Additionally, facilities on Indian campuses are often not suitable for foreign students, with dorms and cafeterias offering standards of living below those to which some international students are accustomed.

India also has not been proactive in attracting international students, and its coordination, communication, and recruitment strategies are weak. Most institutions recruit foreign students themselves, though some universities coordinate recruitment for affiliated colleges. The coordination mechanism for promotion of Indian higher education abroad put in place by the University Grants Commission in 2004/05 has failed to take off. EdCIL (formerly Educational Consultants India Limited) is the coordinating agency for the admission of foreign nationals and overseas Indians, but it recruits less than a thousand students each year. Another thousand come through the Indian Council for Cultural Relations, the public diplomacy arm of the government.

Although India currently hosts only a small number of international students, the consistent increase since 1998/99 is an indication of the country's desire and potential to emerge as an important host nation. In recent years, the government has taken steps to attract international students, including the streamlining of the visa process and the granting of multientry visas for long-term courses. Universities have been advised to set up international student centers, special websites, familiarization sessions, and periodic monitoring of foreign students.

The government plans to set up five universities to cater to the needs of overseas Indian students, with half of the seats reserved for them. The first such university at Bangalore would be done in partnership with the Manipal Group by 2010. Several private institutions are aggressively wooing foreign students. For instance, Vellore Institute of Technology hosts several hundred students from China. Several institutions have world-class infrastructure and facilities for foreign students. A few education hubs are coming up that will create such facilities for a group of institutions. The education city at Chandigarh, Sonepat near Delhi, and Lavasa hill town near Mumbai are such initiatives that have the potential to attract large numbers of international students. Developed as a center of excellence for education and research in hospitality and management education, Lavasa has already commenced academic programs.

Attracting a larger number of international students is important for India. While inbound student mobility might not be a significant source of revenue (except for a few institutions), economist Kaushik Basu has noted that "being a centre of education can also be a source of global influence and soft power" (Basu, 2009). Other benefits could be benchmarking of standards for quality control purposes, stimulating course innovation, enriching cultural and intellectual life, and creating an environment conducive to increased international understanding.

There is no reason for India not to attract as many or a larger number of international students than China—the language of instruction is mostly English, and India's capacity to absorb foreign students is comparable to that of China. However, international student recruitment in India will likely be driven by private providers and not by the state as in China; thus, it might take longer.

Three recent developments suggest that India could possibly attract a larger number of international students. First, in several key host countries, foreign students already constitute a large percentage of total enrollments—in Australia (21.1 percent), the UK (15.8 percent), Sweden (19 percent), Singapore (20 percent), and others.

Further growth in such countries might not be sustainable. Second, there has been a rapid increase in tuition fees in the UK and Australia in recent years, and countries like Germany and France have introduced tuition fees for foreign students. Over the past 25 years, the average college tuition and fees in the U.S. have risen by 440 percent—more than four times the rate of inflation and almost twice the rate of medical care (Cronin & Horton, 2009). As a result, students from low-income families are likely to look for more affordable alternatives.

Finally, study abroad programs in nontraditional destinations are likely to become more popular among students from advanced countries. These countries place a premium on creativity and innovation to stay competitive and have begun to understand that experiences abroad are critical for creative output (Maddux & Galinsky, 2009). This would increase demand for short-term courses as well as longer-term programs. Thus, India has the potential to become an important host country of international students seeking different and enriching experiences.

Foreign Provision in India

The issue of permitting foreign institutions to operate in India has been fiercely debated for over a decade now, even though there is not any significant presence of independent foreign institutions in India. Several foreign providers, such as Sylvan Learning Systems, Carnegie Mellon University, and the Illinois Institute of Technology, have entered India over the past decade and already closed their operations due to unpredictable regulatory complications (Agarwal, 2008b).

In many cases, however, foreign institutions offer programs with Indian partners, mostly domestic private players. These function outside the purview of the regulatory system. A recent study (Dhar, 2008) has identified 143 Indian institutions and 161 foreign education providers engaged in offering academic programs through collaborative arrangements. A total number of 230 collaborations offering 641 programs were noted. Assuming that some of these collaborations were not included in the study, it is estimated that about 29,000 to 48,000 students are enrolled in these programs.

These arrangements would account for about 0.3 percent of total higher education enrollment, but the fees paid by students and parents for these programs amount to a whopping $100 million, or about 5 percent of what the government spends on higher education. Surprisingly, a majority (78 percent) of these students come from middle-income families with an annual income of less than $12,500. In many cases, households spend almost half their annual income on their child's tuition fees to attend these programs. Interestingly, while most Indian institutions are private (77 percent, with two-thirds of these private nonaffiliated), the foreign institutions are public institutions.

The largest numbers of foreign partner institutions are based in the UK (55) and the U.S. (46), followed by Australia. These collaborative arrangements primarily offer undergraduate degree or diploma programs in skill-oriented areas such as business and management studies, engineering and computer applications, and hotel management. Almost all of these programs (88 percent) are offered through face-to-face delivery, with the remaining offered through distance or online delivery models. Incidentally, such arrangements are not explicitly covered in the law currently under debate that would permit foreign providers to operate in India.

The national government has been considering the Foreign Educational Institutions Bill for over three years now. Strong reservations and disagreements have so far prevented its passage. An earlier draft bill brought foreign providers under the regulatory control of the UGC by treating them as deemed universities and subjecting them to fee regulations and quotas in admissions. This has been significantly revised under the new national government that took office in June 2009. The revised bill exempts foreign providers from fee regulations and quotas in admissions and removes them from regulatory oversight by the UGC. However, such institutions would need to have at least 10 years' experience and accreditation from recognized agencies in their own countries (Kasturi, 2009).

The bill in its current form is likely to face opposition, but if passed it will settle a long-pending issue. While media reports state that about 50 foreign universities, including prestigious ones like the U.S.-based Duke University, have indicated interest in setting up campuses in India, the actual level of interest will depend on the final law and the institutional mechanisms set up to implement it. Some independent academics are, however, apprehensive and see hope of foreign investment in higher education "a misleading mirage that disregards reality" (Anandakrishnan, 2006).

Currently, almost all delivery of foreign degrees in India takes place through some form of partnership with an Indian provider, usually in the private sector. These arrangements remain outside the purview of the law under consideration; thus, the uncertainty about the operations of foreign providers in India is likely to continue. Overall, foreign provision in India is currently an extension of private provision and is peripheral to overall higher education provision in the country. Since indecision surrounding the future of foreign institutions emanates from polarized views over the role of private providers more generally, a satisfactory resolution could pave the way for a more liberal regime for private providers in the country as domestic private providers demand to be treated on a par with foreign private providers.

Interestingly, several Indian institutions, mainly private, have set up bases abroad, mainly in Singapore, Dubai, and Malaysia. These destinations aspire to become regional education hubs and host a large number of Indian students. Such operations cater to the local student population in the host country as well as to Indian students. So far, the issue of quality assurance and recognition of qualifications offered by Indian institutions abroad has not surfaced, but as enrollments increase, this will be a critical issue.

Conclusion

India is a key nation in debates surrounding internationalization of higher education. The country's large number of young people, rapidly growing economy, and booming middle class make it a favorite source country among host countries hoping to recruit internationally mobile students. And though India currently only hosts a small number of international students, the country has the potential to host many more. Thus, India's importance in international student mobility is destined to grow.

Currently, foreign provision in India is small and peripheral. Many institutions are keenly watching developments in India related to the new law for foreign providers, and there is a great deal of enthusiasm among foreign universities. India is seen as a huge market with immense potential. Foreign providers can not only create additional capacity but also energize local institutions, both by example and through competition. Thus, opening Indian higher education to foreign competition will strengthen it and boost internationalization efforts.

REFERENCES

Agarwal, P. (2009). *Indian higher education: Envisioning the future*. New Delhi: Sage.

Agarwal, P. (2008a). Privatization and internationalization of higher education in the countries of South Asia: An empirical analysis. Retrieved April 22, 2009 from http://www.saneinetwork.net/pdf/SANEI_VIII/7.pdf

Agarwal, P. (2008b). India in the context of international student circulation. In H. De Wit (Ed.), *The dynamics of international student circulation in a global context* (pp. 83–112). Rotterdam and Taipei: Sense Publishers.

Anandakrishnan, M. (2006, March 11–24). To ensure quality. *Frontline 23*(5).

Association of Indian Universities. (2009). *International students in Indian universities 2006–2007*. New Delhi: Association of Indian Universities.

Association of Indian Universities. (2007). *Student mobility: International students in Indian universities*. New Delhi: Association of Indian Universities.

Basu, K. (2009, August 1). Graduating to a real soft power. *The Hindustan Times, Kolkata*.

Bhandari, R., & Chow, P. (2008). *Open doors 2008: Report on international educational exchange*. New York: Institute of International Education.

Cronin, J.M., & Horton, H.E. (2009). Will higher education be the next bubble to burst? *Chronicle of Higher Education 55*(37), A56. Retrieved November 9, 2009 from http://chronicle.com/article/Will-Higher-Education-Be-the/44400/

De Wit, H. (2008). The internationalization of higher education in a global context. In H. De Wit (Ed.), *The dynamics of international student circulation in a global context* (pp. 1–7). Rotterdam and Taipei: Sense Publishers.

Dhar, I. (2008, May). *Foreign education providers in India: Report on collaborative arrangements*. UK-India Education and Research Initiative (UKIERI).

Gupta, A. (2006, January–March). India's soft power. *Indian Foreign Affairs Journal 1*(1), 45–57.

Kasturi, C.S. (2009, September 20). Free hand to foreign colleges. *The Telegraph, Kolkata*. Retrieved November 9, 2009 from http://www.telegraphindia.com/1090920/jsp/frontpage/story_11518653.jsp

Lightfoot, L. (2009). More overseas students found. *BBC News*. Retrieved May 15, 2009 from http://news.bbc.co.uk/go/pr/fr/-/2/hi/uk_news/education/8060219.stm

Maddux, W.W., & Galinsky, A.D. (2009). Cultural borders and mental barriers: The relationship between living abroad and creativity. *Journal of Personality and Social Psychology 96*(5), 1047–1061.

Rosenzweig, M.R. (2006). *Global wage differences and international student flows*. Retrieved April 24, 2009 from http://www.nyu.edu/africahouse/forresearchers/africana/Mig120506Rosensweig.pdf

Shukla, R.K., Dwivedi, S.K., & Sharma, A. (2004). *The great Indian middle class: Results from the NCAER market information survey of households*. New Delhi: National Council of Applied Economic Research.

United Nations Population Division. (2008). *World population prospects, 2008 revision*. New York: United Nations. Retrieved June 15, 2009 from http://esa.un.org/unpp/

Chapter Five

IS THERE A ROLE FOR FOREIGN PROVIDERS IN INDIA? PAST CHALLENGES AND CURRENT DEVELOPMENTS

SUDHANSHU BHUSHAN, PROFESSOR AND HEAD, DEPARTMENT OF HIGHER AND PROFESSIONAL EDUCATION, NATIONAL UNIVERSITY OF EDUCATIONAL PLANNING AND ADMINISTRATION, NEW DELHI

Internationalization of higher education is acquiring importance in India as more programs promote student and scholar mobility. Cross-border education is also gaining momentum in many other countries, and scholars in this field have examined the phenomenon from many angles—definitions, modes of delivery, providers and partners, nature of courses, rationales and implications, trends, and more (Altbach, 2007; Knight, 2006, 2007). These studies have described challenges related to registration and licensing, quality assurance, accreditation, and recognition of qualifications, with the goal of making these practices meaningful and beneficial in the new context of globalization. Knight proposes a definition of internationalization as "the process of integrating an international, intercultural or global dimension into the purpose, functions or delivery of higher education" (Knight, 2004, p. 9). Knight's proposed "integrationist" definition, however, fails to take account of the disparities that exist between nations or groups of nations. Altbach notes that "[t]he world of globalized higher education is highly unequal" (2007, p. 124). Altbach's "dependency" approach categorizes universities based on their location in either the global center or periphery—the former referring to the research-oriented universities of the North, and the latter to the universities of the South, which depend to a large extent on the centers of research in the North.

Notwithstanding the different approaches represented by Knight and Altbach, the role of foreign providers in any case needs to be seen in the context of economic globalization. This viewpoint supports the idea that economic forces are the dominant factor explaining the rise of foreign education providers in India. These economic forces include privatization and fiscal stringency, and they began to operate with respect to higher education in India after the 1995 General Agreement on Trade in Services (GATS). The influence of economic forces on Indian higher education continued to operate during the subsequent Doha Round of World Trade Organization (WTO) negotiations, which began in 2001 and continues today.

Directing these market forces so that they result in meaningful higher education partnerships is the most difficult challenge that many national higher education systems face today. The case of India offers an interesting perspective on how autonomous (unilateral) liberalization has played out with respect to the higher education sector. Policy makers are increasingly realizing that they need to respond to the present situation by encouraging the internationalization of higher education, and a bill related to foreign universities is currently under active consideration by the Ministry of Human Resource Development, the Indian ministry that deals with education.

In order to understand education policy, we must consider the ideological, economic, social, and political factors that influence decision making (Ball, 1997; Kogan, 1975; Lawton, 1992, 1994; Ozga, 2000; and Phillips, 2003). Considering these factors allows us to apply social science to examine why certain policies have come into effect. With respect to liberalization, the issue of how an expanded role for foreign capital affects the provision of higher education in India suggests the following questions: How is globalization impacting the priority sectors dealing with social welfare, and particularly education policy? What fiscal factors are involved? Is the privatization of higher education primarily a response to changing market conditions? What has been the government response to complex social, political, and economic factors?

This chapter aims to describe the process and factors that led to the emergence of foreign education providers in India. It argues that economic factors were mainly responsible for the autonomous liberalization of higher education in India. Secondly, the chapter attempts to describe the current practices of foreign providers of higher education. Who are these foreign providers? Who are their Indian partners? What programs are being offered and what are their delivery mechanisms? What is the prospective demand for these services? How has this phenomenon been received in Indian academia? What are the proposed regulations with respect to the entry of foreign providers, and what is their intended purpose? Lastly, the chapter looks at current developments and the way forward for the entry of foreign education providers in India.

The Emerging Context of Liberalization in Higher Education

Globalization

The present phase of globalization is characterized by the intense struggle to acquire knowledge and disseminate it in a manner that provides opportunities to earn profits. Institutions of higher education play an important role in these complex dynamics of knowledge production and distribution. Internationalization of higher education—of which program and institutional mobility are key components—deals precisely with these dynamics (Bhushan, 2009). Developing countries often view the internationalization of higher education as an opportunity to participate in the global labor market. Developed countries, in contrast, have well-financed universities that focus on research and teaching. Altbach notes "the powerful universities and academic systems—the centers—have always dominated the production and distribution of knowledge ... smaller and weaker institutions ... have tended to be dependent on them" (Altbach, 2007, p. 124). Thus, the demand in developing countries for international higher education, which is seen to offer graduates an advantage in the labor market, provides the rationale for institutions and programs to move from the center to the periphery. Policy makers in the Indian government cannot ignore the fact that Indian students prefer name-brand foreign universities and that, given the perceived global labor-market advantage of a foreign education and the relatively few places available at high-quality Indian institutions, students who can afford to pay high tuition fees will likely go abroad to study.

General Agreement on Trade in Services

The General Agreement on Trade in Services (GATS) situates educational services in terms of trade. During the Doha Round, the Indian Ministry of Commerce requested that the Ministry of Human Resource Development finalize its recommendations for how to include higher education in the GATS negotiations, which led to intense discussions on the implications of commitment to GATS. Subsequently, the Ministry of Human Resource Development appointed two committees, one on requests and one on offers, to give final recommendations. The government communicated its offers to the WTO, which permitted the entry of foreign providers into India subject to regulations. Though the Doha round of negotiations has not yet concluded, many feel that creating a regulatory environment that allows foreign education providers into India is an urgent priority. Hence, from 2005 to 2006 GATS was instrumental in giving a boost to the liberalization process.

Fiscal Compulsion

In real terms, public expenditure per student in Indian higher education has declined in recent years from $187 in 1993/94 to $130 in 2006/07. Fiscal constraint in financing quality improvements and expansion of higher education has been an important factor in the move toward easing restrictions on the fees that institutions may charge. This deregulated fee structure had already existed in private higher education institutions, which have constituted the main source of expansion in Indian higher education in recent years. Deregulated fee structures were gradually introduced in government and government-aided institutions in the form of self-financing programs. As a result, market forces became more dominant in higher education. Given fiscal constraints, decision makers began to allow more foreign direct investment (FDI). The current policy of the Indian government on FDI in education allows new educational enterprises to be financed entirely by private foreign capital, thus easing the entry of foreign universities.

Privatization

It is interesting to note that privatization of higher education in India was an unsupervised process. A university with degree-granting power can only be established by federal or provincial legislation, resulting in strict barriers to entry. In such a scenario, one way to expand private professional colleges is to affiliate them with existing provincial universities. This is possible because of the particular structure of Indian universities. It is necessary for a college to affiliate with a university in order to admit and teach students. Examinations are conducted at the level of the university, and the affiliated colleges award degrees to successful students.

Almost three-quarters of all professional colleges in the fields of engineering and technology, medical and health sciences, management, and teacher education are private. However, the autonomy of these colleges with regard to admissions and fees has been subject to restrictions imposed by the provincial university. As a result, private providers wanted to have university status. This became possible because the University Grants Commission (UGC) had a provision to allow these institutions and colleges to have university status for certain operations even without following the legislative route. The number of such institutions, known as "private deemed universities," doubled from 2002 to 2007, reaching a total of 104. Additionally, the number of private universities established under provincial legislation went from zero to 40 from 2002 to 2009.

This tremendous growth of private institutions provides a potential basis for collaboration with foreign universities. Yet in the absence of any regulation, "other" private institutions—not categorized under legitimate categories such as colleges affiliated to provincial universities, private deemed universities, or private universities established under provincial legislation—have been established to provide certificates and diplomas. It is this category of "other" private institutions that finds it lucrative to collaborate with foreign universities and institutions for degree or diploma programs. "Other" private providers were left unregulated for over a decade and thus were free to collaborate with foreign universities/institutions, leaving the government in a precarious situation. The National Knowledge Commission recommended minimizing barriers to entry in its 2006 report to the Prime Minister on higher education, nearly providing a free hand to private providers in India. Thus, almost completely unsupervised privatization has been an important factor leading to the autonomous liberalization of higher education in India.

Social and Political Dynamics

It is important to note that economic forces shaping the process of liberalization do not always find favor from a social point of view. Social groups and their corresponding political representatives often oppose liberalization in the education sector on grounds of affordability. Because of stiff opposition from left-wing parties allied with the Congress Party under the United Progressive Alliance (UPA) government, the bill permitting entry and regulation of foreign education providers drafted in 2004 and subsequently modified in 2005 and 2007 was not tabled in the upper house of Parliament. The UPA government completed its term in early 2009, and since the new Congress-led government does not require the support of the parties that had previously opposed the draft bill, the road is almost clear for the government to pass it with whatever modifications the government might introduce. As of this writing, the delay in decision making now seems to be almost over under the commitment to present the bill to the upper house as soon as possible following the beginning of the next session of Parliament.

Thus, globalization, privatization, and fiscal vulnerability created conditions causing the state to lose a portion of its autonomy. More broadly, the government finds it increasingly difficult to fulfill its commitment to expand and improve social sectors such as health and education. The emergence of foreign education providers in India needs to be understood against this background.

Emergence of Foreign Providers

Are Branch Campuses a Possibility?

There are now a few empirical studies on the emergence of foreign education providers in India (Powar & Bhalla, 2006; Bhushan, 2006; British Council, 2008). It may be noted that, aside from a claim made by Western International University, there is no offshore campus of any foreign university in India. However, attempts to open offshore campuses have occurred in the past and continue today. In 2003, Sylvan International Universities (later Laureate Education, Inc.), a U.S. for-profit network of universities, opened an "interim" campus in Hyderabad but discontinued operations following unfavorable regulatory conditions (Observatory on Borderless Higher Education [OBHE], 2004). The Georgia Institute of Technology plans to open a campus once the foreign provider's bill is enacted in the Parliament of India (OBHE, 2007), and Macquarie University in Sydney (Australia) has also announced plans to open a number of campuses in India (Times Higher Education Supplement [THES], 2007).

Despite the intentions of these few universities planning to open a campus in India, it is not immediately clear if the world's most respected research universities will be inspired to open campuses if given clearance from the government. The issue of investment, autonomy, faculty recruitment and remuneration, delivery mechanisms, outflow of capital, and above all how the institutions' nonprofit status will be considered will need to be settled. There is, however, a possibility for respected universities to launch programs in India collaboratively, and such opportunities need to be explored.

Articulation and Twinning

Quite a few foreign universities, including well-regarded ones, are interested in attracting Indian students to their own home campuses while also forging overseas partnerships with Indian institutions by entering into articulation and twinning arrangements with Indian partners. Such overseas institutions recognize and grant specific credit and advanced standing to applicants from a program of study pursued at the Indian institution (Academic Cooperation Association, 2008). The foreign institution provides the course material to the Indian partner or agrees to accept the partner's own course as an alternative. Under twinning arrangements, one part of the program of study is completed at the foreign or overseas institution. Indian students are eager to avail themselves of such partnerships as they allow them to pursue part of their education abroad and to receive certification from foreign universities, credentials that provide a competitive edge in the labor market.

The University of Lancashire (United Kingdom) has articulation arrangements with Indira School of Communication in Pune (BA Hons. in international journalism) and with the Asian Academy of Film and Television in Noida (various programs including cinema, mass communication, radio, and television). The last year is spent at the foreign campus, and candidates are recruited by a visiting team. Powar and Bhalla (2006) found that 20 universities/institutions from the UK, 17 from the U.S., 9 from Australia, and 4 from Canada are engaged in articulation agreements in India, mostly with private commercial institutions.

Articulation leads to twinning. It is important to note that credit transfer and articulation agreements are not very popular in the Indian university system, and only a few "other" private providers engage with foreign universities in articulation agreements that lead to a foreign higher education degree for Indian students.

Franchising

In addition to attracting students to home campuses, foreign providers deliver programs through franchising. Under franchising agreements, the foreign (home) institution licenses a host institution to teach some or all of its courses so that students can receive the credential of the foreign institution without attending classes at the foreign campus. This is a form of international outsourcing in which some of the activities normally provided by the franchiser are contracted out to the local partner institution (McBurnie & Ziguras, 2007). The foreign institution holds overall responsibility for program content, delivery, assessment, and quality assurance. Foreign providers include many established universities and also commercial establishments without reliable academic credentials. As of 2006, there were 23 universities/institutions from the UK, 15 from the U.S., and 11 from Canada according to the estimate of Powar and Bhalla (2006). Regulatory authorities in India do not look favorably on franchising, and the regulations of the All India Council for Technical Education (AICTE) forbid franchising in technical education.

The above classification system may not cover all methods for delivery of educational services in India. In some cases, the foreign institution provides the complete course to the local partner. The local partner delivers the course, and the foreign institution monitors academic standards. Occasionally, agencies may just prepare Indian students for entry into a particular degree program in the foreign country. Sometimes a single degree is awarded, and sometimes these arrangements lead to a dual or joint degree. There may also be blended learning—for example, e-learning delivered via software or the Internet is combined with face-to-face learning. If we group these additional delivery methods under the category of "foreign education provider," this category becomes much broader.

British Council Study Estimates

In 2008, the British Council carried out a detailed study of foreign education providers in India. The study identified 143 Indian institutions and 161 foreign education providers, with significant numbers from the UK (55) and the U.S. (46) engaged in offering academic programs through collaborative arrangements. The study identified 230 collaborations offering 641 programs. Further, the study estimated that 29,000 to 48,000 students were enrolled in collaborative programs in India, though this may be an overestimate. Taking a weighted average of the cost per student of all the collaborative programs in India, the annual fee comes to US$2,500, which compares with average fees of US$419 in federal universities, US$682 in provincial universities, and US$1,300 in private deemed universities where tuition and fees are not subsidized and where students pay the full cost of courses. The study also found that a significant proportion of students studying in such courses (60 percent) were from households whose total annual income fell in the range of US$4,300 to US$13,000. These fees, then, range from 20 to 50 percent of total per capita income, indicating that a large urban middle class with ambitions to participate in the global labor market is willing to pay for such foreign programs. The most common specializations of collaborative arrangements, according to the British Council study, were undergraduate degree or diploma programs in vocational fields such as business and management studies, engineering and computer applications, and hotel management.

One such example is that of the Wigan & Leigh College India (WLCI), a network of campuses affiliated with Wigan & Leigh College in the UK, which is situated in over 40 locations in India and offers more than 20 professional diploma and certificate programs in areas including hospitality, insurance, banking, media, and advertising. All these courses are recognized by Wigan & Leigh, UK.

Ansal Institute of Technology (AIT) claims that 12 of its undergraduate programs and 5 of its graduate programs are recognized by 9 universities in the U.S., 3 in Canada, and 4 in Australia. Over 600 AIT students have been accepted by reputable universities in the U.S., Australia, and Canada in the last few years through twinning arrangements involving credit transfer (Ansal Institute of Technology).

L.N. Welingkar Institute of Management Development & Research, Mumbai has twinning programs with Nottingham Trent University, UK, in the field of bioinformatics. The MSc Bioinformatics is a one-year program of 180 credit points, of which 90 credit points are earned through courses at Welingkar during the first six months, and the additional 90 credit points are earned through studies at Nottingham Trent University in the final six months. The final degree is awarded jointly by both institutions.

Private Partners in India

The 2008 British Council study found that 82 percent of Indian institutions collaborating with foreign universities and institutions are in the private sector. There are very few public universities and institutions collaborating with foreign education providers. The study distinguishes three categories of private partners in India. The first category is institutions affiliated with universities (29 percent). Sreenidhi Institute of Science and Technology, Hyderabad, is affiliated with Jawaharlal Nehru Technological University, Hyderabad. Institute of Computer and Business Management-School of Business Excellence, Hyderabad, is affiliated with Osmania University, Hyderabad. Skyline Education Group, Delhi, is a branch campus of Manipal Academy of Higher Education, Manipal (a private deemed university). These private institutions, after affiliating themselves with Indian universities, have engaged in collaborations with foreign universities and awarded foreign degrees.

The second category of Indian partner consists of private nonaffiliated institutions (48 percent). These institutions deliver different kinds of programs, such as insurance and finance, hotel management, and hospitality management. Most are not recognized by any university established by an Indian Act, so they remain outside the purview of formal higher education.

The third category is that of private companies (5 percent). A few examples are Raffles Design International, Mumbai; Wigan & Leigh College, Delhi; and Frankfinn Institute of Air Hostess Training, Mumbai. These are established under the Companies Act and collaborate with foreign institutions to award foreign degrees.

The second and third private provider categories do not generally offer degree-granting programs, as they are not affiliated with any of the universities that make up the Indian higher education system. Together, they account for 53 percent of all programs in India delivered through collaboration with foreign partners, and they conduct various diploma programs. They make various arrangements with foreign universities, including twinning, franchising, validation, and articulation, so some of their students do have the chance to earn a foreign degree.

Discipline under Collaborative Partnership

The majority of foreign education providers offer professional and/or vocational courses. Out of the total sample of 131 institutions, 107 provided vocational training, 19 provided technical training, and only five offered general education courses. The data show that in the category of vocational courses, management courses were the most common. Business management and hotel management constituted approximately 80 percent of the total provision (Bhushan, 2006).

Vocational courses offered by private providers in collaboration with foreign institutions are reported to be popular, because they offer promising employment prospects in the private sector upon graduation even though they are not officially recognized in India. It would be fair to conclude that foreign institutions offer a very narrow range of programs in India and that their programs are concentrated in revenue-generating subject areas.

Other Interesting Features

A 2005 study by the National University of Educational Planning and Administration (NUEPA) observed that twinning arrangements with Indian institutions are the most popular type of collaborative arrangement between foreign and Indian universities. Foreign universities encourage twinning because this arrangement leads Indian students to pursue a portion of their studies at the foreign institution. Institutional mobility, however, is nonexistent so far. Foreign institutions have not made the minimum investments in infrastructure and faculty development that are necessary to commit to an offshore campus. At the present time, therefore, foreign institutions have little to lose. The majority of Indian partners are in the private sector. The basic motive of these partner institutions is to earn revenue, and institutional mechanisms to assure quality and provide recognition and equivalence are not in place. Many foreign institutions offer programs accredited in their own countries or by international accreditation agencies, but this does not necessarily ensure that the collaborative program will be a quality one. It is important to note that Indian private institutions' zeal is responsible for the growth in the number of foreign education providers, who have demonstrated an equal willingness to tap into the market. Some of the programs of private institutions in India are recognized by a state government or AICTE. The same private institutions often have an additional agreement with the foreign institution to deliver a foreign degree through twinning or another mode. The size of the market is large since the demand for quality higher education by the upper middle class in India is unmet under the present system.

Views of Academia and Proposed Legislation

The information presented above shows that the provision of programs by private providers in collaboration with foreign universities is far less prevalent in India than internationalization trends elsewhere in the world would indicate. The rising incomes of the Indian upper middle class, the pursuit of foreign degrees, and the desire for upward economic mobility have generated a large demand for lucrative and market-oriented courses. Private providers with their sights on this market have found ways to supply programs with promising job prospects—postsecondary professional programs leading to diplomas or certificates. A degree program is also delivered wherever possible, either in collaboration with universities in India or with foreign universities. The very concept of internationalization has become increasingly diffuse as a result of these arrangements. Advanced degree programs grounded in solid theoretical knowledge and delivered by respected foreign universities are nearly nonexistent in India since the regulatory environment so far has not created a structural space for such programs. The system does not yet allow for recognition of qualifications offered by foreign providers or for the integration of transnational higher education into the country's domestic regulatory framework (Bhushan, 2006).

Altbach (2008) captures current practices very aptly when he writes that "[u]ninformed or simply avaricious institutions in developing countries may form partnerships with low-quality colleges and universities in, for example, the U.S., Australia, and the UK, and receive substandard teaching or degree courses.... There are not enough top-quality universities in countries such as China and India to absorb all the potential overseas partners." There are also concerns that top-class research universities in the U.S., the UK, and Australia are accustomed to working in an environment in their respective countries that they will have difficulty replicating in India, adding to the challenge of attracting enough funds to operate a branch campus.

Challenging the Underlying Assumptions

A consultative meeting organized by the National University of Educational Planning and Administration on Foreign Providers in Indian Higher Education stressed the need for collaboration. However, it pointed out a few misconceptions related to foreign education programs in India (NUEPA, 2009). These include the following:

1. Allowing foreign universities to operate in India does not guarantee that outward mobility of students will decline.

2. Allowing foreign universities to operate in India does not guarantee that programs in India will be cheaper than programs delivered abroad. They are likely to charge heavily for curricula, teaching, and other guidance delivered through collaborative programs.

3. Foreign universities do not necessarily provide quality education.

4. Foreign universities will not necessarily operate as brick-and-mortar campuses.

5. Foreign universities will be least interested in setting up branch campuses.

Although the NUEPA report has been submitted to the Indian government, it is not yet clear whether the government will act on the proposed recommendations.

Prospective Legislation

The Indian government has attempted to pass legislation on the entry of foreign educational institutions into the country since 2004. A 2007 proposed draft of the bill was prepared by the Ministry of Human Resource Development and discussed by a ministerial committee. So far, this bill has not been introduced in any of the houses of Parliament. As the proposed draft states, any foreign educational institution willing to provide a degree or diploma through an overseas campus will have to apply under the procedures specified in the act. Foreign universities' credentials should be well established. The present draft of the bill grants more control to the government and aims to prevent commercialization. No foreign institution is allowed to repatriate any part of the surplus earned, and any surplus must be invested in expansion or quality improvement. Collaboration, partnership, and twinning arrangements have been kept outside the purview of the bill. The present draft provides little autonomy to the foreign institutions. No private or reputable research university is expected to invest under the provisions of the bill, but discussions on the draft bill are still continuing.

Ways Forward

The present practices are guided by market forces, and regulations need to be put in place to allow for the development of quality programs by foreign providers in India. However, it is challenging to create incentives for the credible public higher education system in India to collaborate with reputable universities abroad to launch joint programs of teaching and research. Curricula and course development, innovative teaching, mentoring the faculty, and evaluation of programs should be of central importance in these collaborative partnerships. Overall, an academic environment that encourages the creative engagement of students and teachers should emerge as an important objective of the internationalization of higher education in India.

The question of whether the world's reputable research universities will wish to pursue collaborations in India depends on the leadership of Indian universities and their departments, and also on central government policy. Rather than controlling and over-regulating from the center, the government should allow for greater academic freedom at individual universities. Accredited and reputable foreign universities should be permitted to collaborate for delivery of degree-granting and nondegree joint programs. Such collaboration should take place with government and government-aided universities and colleges, and should deliver joint degrees. Such collaboration could also take place with private universities and colleges under strict guidelines from the University Grants Commission to prevent commercialization. The government needs to provide the academic freedom necessary for institutions to jointly run the programs under the broad UGC guidelines.

Indian higher education suffers from a quality and relevance gap in relation to higher education in developed countries. Indian universities need to bridge this gap and work towards making India an education hub by attracting top scholars to teach and conduct research in the country. This is possible only if reputable research universities are allowed to enter under mutually beneficial terms. Universities in India should be encouraged to make collaborative alliances, and the government should be ready to provide adequate funds to manage such partnerships. It is within this framework that the role of foreign education providers in India should be envisioned.

REFERENCES

Academic Cooperation Association. (2008, July). *Transnational education in the European context - provision, approaches, and policies.* Retrieved November 9, 2009 from http://ec.europa.eu/education/erasmus-mundus/doc1408_en.htm

Altbach, P. (2008, February 14). The "global market" bubble. Times Higher Education Supplement.

Altbach, P. (2007). Globalization and the university: Realities in an unequal world. In J. Forest & P. Altbach (Eds.), International handbook of higher education (pp. 65–82). Dordrecht, The Netherlands: Springer.

Ansal Institute of Technology. International collaborations. Retrieved November 9, 2009 from http://www.aitgurgaon.org/AboutUs/AcademicLinkages1.html

Ball, S. (1997). Markets, equity and values in education. In R. Pring & G. Walford (Eds.), Affirming the comprehensive ideal (pp. 69–82). London: Falmer.

Bhushan, S. (2009, July). Internationalisation of higher education: Developing countries' perspective. Paper presented at the meeting of the World Conference on Higher Education UNESCO, Paris.

Bhushan, S. (2006, March). Foreign education providers in India: Mapping the extent and regulation. The Observatory on Borderless Higher Education - Observatory reports.

British Council. (2008). Foreign education providers in India: Report on collaborative arrangements. New Delhi, India: British Council.

Knight, J. (2007). Internationalization: Concepts, complexities and challenges. In J. Forest & P. Altbach (Eds.), International handbook of higher education (pp. 207–208). Dordrecht, The Netherlands: Springer.

Knight, J. (2006). Crossborder education: An analytical framework for program and provider mobility. In J.C. Smart (Ed.), Higher education: Handbook of theory and research, 21 (pp. 345–396). Dordrecht, The Netherlands: Springer.

Knight, J. (2004). Internationalization remodeled: Rationales, strategies and approaches. Journal for Studies in International Education, 8(1), 5–31.

Kogan, M. (1975). Educational policy-making: A study of interest groups and Parliament. London: Allen and Unwin.

Lawton, D. (1992). Education and politics in the 1990s: Conflict or consensus? London: The Falmer Press.

Lawton, D. (1994). The Tory mind on education, 1979–1994. London: The Falmer Press.

McBurnie, G., & Ziguras, C. (2007). Transnational education: Issues and trends in offshore higher education. London and New York: Routledge.

National Knowledge Commission. (2006, November 29). Note on higher education. Retrieved November 9, 2009 from http://www.knowledgecommission.gov.in/downloads/recommendations/HigherEducationLetterPM.pdf

National University of Educational Planning and Administration. (2009). Report on national consultation on foreign providers in Indian higher education: Issues of entry, regulation and models of engagement. Unpublished manuscript, NUEPA, New Delhi, India

National University of Educational Planning and Administration. (2005). A research report on foreign education providers in India. New Delhi: NUEPA.

Observatory on Borderless Higher Education. (2007, June 20). A careful and timely vision? US-based Georgia Institute of Technology eyes a branch campus in India. OBHE Breaking News. Retrieved November 9, 2009 from http://www.obhe.ac.uk/documents/view_details?id=171

Observatory on Borderless Higher Education. (2004, January 28). Sylvan closes India campus citing lack of co-operation from UGC: A victory for quality or confusion? OBHE Breaking News. Retrieved November 9, 2009 from http://www.obhe.ac.uk/documents/view_details?id=479

Ozga, J. (2000). Policy research in educational settings: Contested terrain. Buckingham, UK: Open University Press.

Phillips, R. (2003). Education policy, comprehensive schooling and devolution in the disUnited Kingdom: An historical "home international" analysis. Journal of Education Policy, 18(1), 1–17.

Powar, K.B., & Bhalla, V. (2006). Foreign providers of higher education in India: Realities, implications and options. Pune, India: D. Y. Patil University.

Times Higher Education Supplement. (2007, April 27). Macquarie plans Indian off-shoots. Times Higher Education Supplement.

Chapter Six

AMERICA'S NEW IMMIGRANT ENTREPRENEURS

VIVEK WADHWA, EXECUTIVE IN RESIDENCE, PRATT SCHOOL OF ENGINEERING
AT DUKE UNIVERSITY

Vinod Khosla was born in Pune, India, in 1955. His father, an officer in the Indian Army, had no business background. But young Vinod gravitated towards entrepreneurship from an early age. When he was 16, Vinod first read about Intel and the microprocessor revolution. The possibilities of the technology electrified him. Vinod began dreaming of launching his own computer or technology company. An excellent math and science student, Vinod gained entry to the rigorous electrical engineering program at the vaunted Indian Institute of Technology (IIT), Delhi. Twenty-year-old Vinod's first venture, a soy milk company, quickly failed due to a fact that should have been obvious in hindsight: most residents of India did not have refrigerators back then.

Vinod instead went to the U.S. and received a Master in Biomedical Engineering degree at Carnegie Mellon University and then an MBA from Stanford University. Upon completion of his MBA in 1980, Khosla founded Daisy Computers with two co-founders. The company was among the first to make computer-aided design tools for electrical engineers. After realizing that he needed a better standardized hardware platform to build on, Khosla joined with Bill Joy, Scott McNealy, and Andreas Bechtolsheim to form Sun Microsystems in 1982. Sun went on to become one of the largest computer companies in the country, and Khosla went on to become one of the world's top venture capitalists, with a hand in founding or funding dozens of companies.

The story of Vinod Khosla is hardly an anomaly. The ranks of America's tech founders are disproportionately filled with Indians, especially when compared to the general U.S. population, of which Indians make up less than one percent. The experience of Indian entrepreneurs in the U.S. is a topic that has come under increasing scrutiny. Of particular note are the support networks that Indians have created to foster entrepreneurship such as The Indus Entrepreneurs, a global organization that has become an invaluable Rolodex to members seeking to launch businesses, receive advice and funding, and find partners and employees. Along with the success of Indian entrepreneurs, the myth of the Indian engineer as a technology virtuoso in the rarified computer-related disciplines of semiconductors, hardware, and software has taken hold in the larger U.S. culture and other parts of the world.

The Expanding Role of Immigrants in U.S. Competitiveness

The context of the rise of the Indian entrepreneur is mirrored, somewhat, by the corresponding rise of the immigrant entrepreneur. In the past two decades, the growth of immigrants as a percentage of the U.S. workforce has been remarkable. Between 1990 and 2007, the proportion of immigrants in the U.S. labor force increased from 9.3 percent to 15.7 percent, according to the U.S. Census. Approximately 45 percent of the growth of the work force over this period consisted of immigrants. They came for the traditional reasons—education, professional opportunities, a chance at a better life. Many of these immigrants brought high levels of education and advanced skills, and as a result, immigrants have contributed disproportionately to the most dynamic part of the U.S. economy—the high-tech sector.

In 1999, AnnaLee Saxenian published a groundbreaking report on the economic contributions of skilled immigrants to California's economy. This study, "Silicon Valley's New Immigrant Entrepreneurs," focused on the development of Silicon Valley's regional economy and the roles of immigrant capital and labor in this process. Saxenian's study went beyond a quantitative analysis to focus on the social, ethnic, and economic networks of new U.S. immigrants.

One of her most interesting findings was that Chinese and Indian engineers ran a growing share of Silicon Valley companies started during the 1980s and 1990s and were at the helm of 24 percent of Silicon Valley technology businesses started from 1980 to 1998. Saxenian concluded that foreign-born scientists and engineers were generating new jobs and wealth for the California economy. Even those who returned to their home countries to take advantage of opportunities there were building links to the U.S. and spurring technological innovation and economic expansion for California.

In follow-up research conducted by my team at Duke University in 2006, we found that the trend that Saxenian had documented had become a nationwide phenomenon. Of all technology and engineering companies founded nationwide between 1995 and 2000, over 25 percent had an immigrant as a chief executive or lead technologist. In Silicon Valley, this number had increased to 52 percent. Immigrants have been co-founders of many prominent firms: Google, eBay, and Yahoo, to name a few.

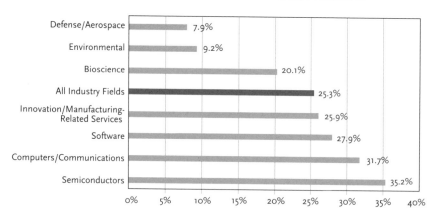

We also found that Indians dominated the group of immigrant entrepreneurs who had founded technology companies. They founded more U.S. engineering and technology companies than immigrants from the UK, China, Taiwan, and Japan combined. Of all immigrant-founded companies, 26 percent have Indian founders. Indian immigrants constituted only .67 percent of the U.S. population in 2000 but started 6.57 percent of all technology and engineering companies from 1995 to 2005.

FIGURE 6.2: ORIGIN OF U.S. IMMIGRANT FOUNDERS

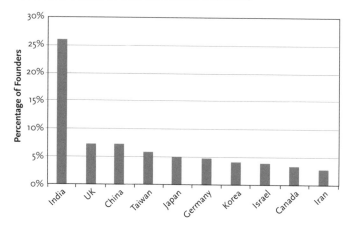

Contributions of Indian-Americans to Global Intellectual Property

In our research we not only tracked the founders of technology companies but also examined the intellectual property contribution of immigrants to the U.S. This is logical because patent filings are closely related to growth of intellectual property (IP) portfolios. By extension, countries with richer IP portfolios have exhibited strong economic performance in fast-growing, profitable sectors like technology and medical devices. And the people who file patents are often among the most innovative leaders and thinkers in science and technology fields.

We studied the World Intellectual Property Organization (WIPO) Patent Cooperation Treaty (PCT) records for the U.S.-originated international patent filings by U.S.-resident inventors. We determined that in 2006, foreign nationals residing in the U.S. were named as inventors or co-inventors in 25.6 percent of WIPO patent applications filed from the U.S.

Foreign nationals contributed a significant majority of all patents submitted by some U.S. companies. For example, immigrant patent filings represented 72 percent of the total at Qualcomm, 65 percent of the total at Merck, 64 percent of the total at General Electric, and 60 percent at Cisco Systems. Over 40 percent of the international patent applications filed by the U.S. government had foreign national authors.

When we examined the name heritage of patent authors, we found some very interesting statistics. In 1998, 9.5 percent of these global patent applications had an inventor or co-inventor with a last name suggesting Indian ancestry. In 2006 this percentage had increased to 13.7 percent. So it appears that Indian immigrants were making a substantial and rapidly increasing contribution to U.S. intellectual property during this time period.

To put these numbers into perspective, it is worth noting that India-born immigrants constitute less than one percent of the U.S. population, and census data show that 81.8 percent of Indian immigrants to the U.S. arrived after 1980 (Reeves & Bennett, 2004, p. 10). So these immigrant groups made a rapid and disproportionate contribution to U.S. intellectual property compared to their population. In other words, they behaved much like Vinod Khosla, who came to the U.S., immersed himself in academic study, emerged to innovate in the technology field, and then became an entrepreneur.

The question became, why are immigrant entrepreneurs, and Indian entrepreneurs in particular, gravitating to the technology field?

Why Did Indian Technologists Come to the U.S.?

The answers are both cultural and historical. Vinod Khosla's family was not of the lower class. But Khosla likely understood the limitations of his future in India in the late seventies. The country's economy was moribund and run largely as an appendage of the quasi-socialist Indian government. Entrepreneurship was not encouraged.

Accumulating wealth was difficult and often accomplished via corruption or nepotism rather than through the launch of a new company. At the same time, India was always an open society. Western media was freely purchased and consumed.

News of exciting developments in Silicon Valley was eagerly consumed by young Indians like Vinod. They could feel a huge groundswell of change emanating from northern California and could see wealth creation in action as large companies in the technology arena began to grow exponentially. For young Indians studying high-tech disciplines such as electrical engineering and computer science, the promise of the U.S. as a place to obtain graduate degrees and later employment became brighter and brighter.

As in Vinod Khosla's case, these were not, by and large, low-class Indians. IIT attendees were mostly middle- to upper-class people, since passing the rigorous entrance exams was difficult even for a well-schooled undergraduate and extremely difficult for undergraduates from backgrounds that offered them fewer opportunities for intense academic exposure. Khosla was the son of an Indian Army officer, for example. Yet these IIT students understood that a better life likely awaited them in America, and not only in terms of remuneration. The U.S. at the time was by far the biggest powerhouse in scientific research, an untouchable ivory tower. Equally important, Khosla and his cohorts saw the U.S. as the best place to bridge those twin desires—for better pay and living standards, and for work that was meaningful, cutting-edge, and intellectually stimulating.

Educational Background of Indian-American Entrepreneurs

Our immigration data showed that immigrant entrepreneurs in general tended to be very highly educated—96 percent held bachelor's degrees and 74 percent held graduate or postgraduate degrees (26.8 percent held PhDs and 47.2 percent held master's degrees). The vast majority (75 percent) of their highest degrees were in science, technology, engineering, and mathematics (STEM) fields: applied sciences (10.2 percent), engineering (43.5 percent), mathematics (2.8 percent), and computer science and information technology (18.5 percent). According to the U.S. census, Indian-Americans are among the highest-educated immigrant groups (Reeves & Bennett, 2004, p. 12).

The opinion of the researchers was that education was a clear differentiator and provided Indian immigrants an advantage. There is, however, a common belief in the U.S. that most Indian entrepreneurs are the graduates of a small cadre of elite institutions in India such as the IITs. Our research showed that this was not the case; that Indian entrepreneurs graduated from a wide assortment of universities, and many of these were lower-tiered schools that are not well known in the U.S. In fact, only 15 percent had received their undergraduate education at one of the seven IIT campuses.

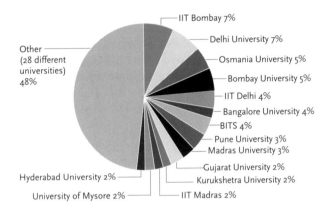

American Education: The Gateway to America

Our research showed that the majority of immigrant founders came to the U.S. as students—52.3 percent of immigrant founders initially came to the U.S. primarily for higher education, 39.8 percent entered the country because of a job opportunity, 5.5 percent came for family reasons, and only 1.6 percent came for entrepreneurship. They ended up staying in the U.S. after graduation and founded companies an average of 13 years after their arrival.

Anecdotal data show that in recent years most foreign students have taken employment in the U.S. after graduating from U.S. colleges. Large proportions of these students end up putting down roots in the U.S. and staying permanently. In his research for the National Science Foundation, Michael Finn found that two-thirds of foreign citizens who received science or engineering doctorates from U.S. universities in 2003 lived in the U.S. in 2005. The five-year stay rate for Indians receiving these degrees was 85 percent.

The success of immigrant Indians created a strong positive feedback loop, with the image of accomplished Indian entrepreneurs in the U.S. enticing even more talented young Indians to come to the U.S. to study and later work. The pull of the U.S. also remained strong because India continued to lag behind many western countries in terms of growth rates and infrastructure development until the earliest years of the twenty-first century. The government in India continued to dominate the commercial sphere. Starting and growing a company in the Subcontinent remained extremely difficult. Yet the seeds of a reversal had already begun to take shape even in the first years of the twenty-first century.

The Seeds of Return

In the final years of the twentieth century, a nascent native Indian technology industry began to take shape. Initially handling the mundane back-office requirements of multinationals, these "body shops" gained a toehold due to the overwhelming labor cost advantage they could bring to bear as compared to cost of comparable employees in the West. At the same time, the rise of a global data communications network made performance of many back-office tasks no longer site-specific. The software and information technology (IT) services industry was allowed to develop relatively unfettered by the Indian government.

By 2000, a handful of Indian firms, including Cognizant, WiPro, and Infosys, had begun to distinguish themselves at home and abroad. They slowly began climbing the IT value chain. Concurrently, many global multinational companies (MNCs) began to recognize the native talent found in India's diverse English-speaking workforce. India's higher education system, while not as strong as those found in the West, turned out significant numbers of quality graduates from programs at both the undergraduate and graduate levels. As a result, large MNCs such as Cisco, General Electric, and others began to set up research shops in India as part of a plan to defray costs and develop products more suited for fast-growing markets in Asia and the developing world.

At the same time, in the U.S. an immigration time-bomb had begun ticking. Restrictive immigration policies left tens of thousands of talented Indian immigrant scientists and technologists in bureaucratic limbo as they awaited their Green Cards, with no guarantee of fulfillment. As the queue grew in the U.S., the magnet of working at home in India grew stronger with each passing year of rapid Indian economic growth. A massive bubble in the U.S. masked the effects of this growing gap by creating numerous high-paying jobs that were open to smart immigrants.

But when that bubble began to burst in 2007, the façade of a fast-growing U.S. economy was laid bare. Young Indians who might have sought to start companies in the U.S. instead began to seriously reconsider whether the proverbial Land of Opportunity was in fact the best place to bet on for future economic growth. Thousands of Indian entrepreneurs also made the decision to return to India, a growing exodus that has altered the perception of young Indian would-be entrepreneurs enrolled in U.S. graduate and professional school programs.

We wanted to learn about this exodus so we ran a survey that included 1,203 Indian and Chinese immigrants who had worked or received education in the U.S. and subsequently returned to their home country. We constructed our sample by locating persons on the LinkedIn website who had U.S. academic degrees or more than one year of U.S. work experience and who, at the time of the survey, were working for Indian and Chinese companies. The survey was conducted over a period of 6 months in 2008. LinkedIn is an online network of more than 30 million experienced professionals and managers from around the world and is a valuable source of information on these types of workers. We obtained a 90 percent response rate on the survey. While our findings cannot be used to generalize for all highly educated returnees, they are representative of the young professionals on the site.

The vast majority of the Indian sample was relatively young, with an average age in the mid-30s. Over 85 percent of Indian respondents had advanced degrees. Professional and educational development opportunities were among the strongest factors bringing these immigrants to the U.S. initially. Interestingly, the move home also appeared to be something of a career catalyst. Respondents reported that they have moved up the organization chart by returning home. The percentage of Indian respondents holding senior management positions increased from 10.2 percent in the U.S. to 44.1 percent in India. Opportunities for professional advancement were considered by 61.1 percent of Indians to be better at home than in the U.S. Most telling of all, 54 percent of Indians who had returned felt that opportunities to launch their own business were significantly better in their home countries.

To be sure, some of the returnees already have plans to go back to the U.S.— 25.3 percent of Indian respondents stated that they were likely to move back. The survey also indicated that offering career opportunities and permanent resident status to Indians who have returned to India would also entice a significant percentage of them to move back to the U.S. If presented with a suitable job in the U.S. and a permanent resident visa, 22.9 percent of Indians said they would return to the U.S., and an additional 39.8 percent said they would consider the offer seriously. So the path of return to India does not appear to be a permanent transfer.

Clearly, asking only those who left skews the data away from revealing positive perceptions of the U.S. The sample pool had already made the decision to leave the U.S. and was therefore predisposed to be more optimistic about the country to which they had chosen to return. But the responses did provide some clear insights into perceptions of the departed. Anecdotally, as well, their expectations of a better economic and career future in India have been borne out in my own observations. When I began teaching in 2004 at Duke University in the Master of Engineering Management program, most of my Indian students sought to stay in the U.S. For the graduating class of 2008, not a single Indian student planned to stay in the U.S.

To get a better read on the intentions of this next generation of Indian entrepreneurs, we developed a survey of foreign students. Specifically, we wanted to learn how they viewed the U.S., how they viewed their home countries, and where they planned to work and live after they graduated. We surveyed 1,224 foreign nationals who were currently studying in institutions of higher learning in the U.S. or who had graduated by the end of the 2008 academic school year. The survey included 229 students from China (and Hong Kong), 117 students from Western Europe, and 878 students from India. This survey was conducted through a contest on Facebook, the social networking website. These data may not be representative of all foreign students, but they provide a snapshot of the views of a fairly large sample.

The overall consensus among Indian respondents was that the U.S. was no longer the destination of choice for careers after graduation. Only 6 percent of Indian respondents said they wanted to stay permanently in the U.S., and 55 percent said they wanted to return home within a few years. Part of this feeing likely arose from concerns over work visas; 85 percent of Indians said they were concerned about obtaining one. The general U.S. economy appeared to be another worry, as 74 percent of Indians were concerned about obtaining jobs in their fields in the U.S. Among Indian respondents, only 25 percent stated they believe the best days of the U.S. economy lie ahead, compared to 86 percent who felt that the best days for the Indian economy lie ahead. Indians were the most positive of the three foreign national groups we surveyed on the economic future of their home country.

From our survey responses, we were able to draw some useful and discouraging conclusions. The period of rapidly rising Indian entrepreneurship in the U.S. appears to be over. Indian students in STEM disciplines who would have stayed on to do postdoctoral work or pursue research in corporate labs in the U.S. are far more likely than ever before to return to India.

As discussed earlier in this chapter, Indians represent very high percentages of the total students in undergraduate and graduate programs in STEM fields. They are also represented disproportionately among the ranks of founding executives at U.S. technology firms around the U.S. So losses of the acorns of entrepreneurship, the young Indians in U.S. higher education, will likely have significant downstream effects on entrepreneurship in high technology fields where Indians have played such a large role.

As our study was not longitudinal, we cannot directly compare the factors influencing the students' decision to stay or leave the U.S. after obtaining a degree, and in the case of students who have already returned to India, we must rely on their recollection of past motivations. Even so, the comparison seems to indicate that significantly more Indian students do not wish to stay in the U.S. than was the norm in the past. In a nutshell, if Vinod Khosla were graduating from Stanford Graduate School of Business today, he would be far more likely to seek a job in India rather than stay on in Silicon Valley.

REFERENCES

Saxenian, A.L. (1999). *Silicon Valley's new immigrant entrepreneurs*. San Francisco: Public Policy Institute of California.

Reeves, T.J., & Bennett, C.E. (2004, December). *We the people: Asians in the United States*. Census 2000 Special Reports. Washington, D.C.: U.S. Census Bureau.

Chapter Seven

INTERCULTURAL COMPETENCE: AN OUTCOME OF STUDENT EXCHANGE

DARLA DEARDORFF, RESEARCH SCHOLAR, DUKE UNIVERSITY

RANJINI MANIAN, FOUNDER AND CEO, GLOBAL ADJUSTMENTS SERVICES

SHOBHA NAIDU, SENIOR MANAGER, CROSS-CULTURAL SERVICES, GLOBAL ADJUSTMENTS BANGALORE

I suppose leadership at one time meant muscles; but today it means getting along with people.
Mahatma Gandhi

Our very survival has never required greater cooperation and understanding among all people from all places than at this moment in history … when we open our hearts and our minds to those who may not think like we do or believe what we do—that's when we discover at least the possibility of common ground.
Barack Obama

Intercultural competence, an often-desired outcome of student exchange, includes elements of the understanding, cooperation, open-mindedness, and common ground of which U.S. President Barack Obama speaks; it also resonates with Gandhi's definition of leadership. With such a broad scope, intercultural competence as a concept raises many fundamental questions: What does it mean to understand each other? What does it mean to open our hearts and minds—to discover the possibility of common ground? What does it truly mean to get along with others? These questions frame this chapter.

As we explore the U.S.-India international higher education relationship, it becomes imperative for us to think more broadly about why such exchange is important and what outcomes we ultimately hope will emerge from these exchanges. One such outcome is the development of students' intercultural competence. Knight (2009) notes that an increased emphasis on developing intercultural competence is a recent trend in higher education. This leads us to more specific questions: What is intercultural competence? From a U.S. perspective? From an Indian perspective? And what are the implications of these definitions as we expand student mobility between the U.S. and India? This chapter begins by discussing key differences between the two cultures before exploring this concept of intercultural competence from both a U.S. and an Indian perspective. Throughout, possible implications of intercultural competence development within student exchange will be woven into the discussion.

Key Cultural Challenges for Students in Indo-U.S. Exchange

Before looking at conceptions of intercultural competence from U.S. and Indian perspectives, it is important to examine briefly the key differences between the two cultures which may present challenges to students involved in U.S.-India exchange and may impede intercultural competence development if not fully considered.

A first-time sojourner to India is often struck by overwhelming first impressions: the extremes of poverty and wealth, the presence of advanced technologies alongside preindustrial ones, excellent schools coexisting with illiteracy, the latest medical facilities available to some but lack of basic care for many—and all of this and more coexisting within a diverse, secular, democratic country of over a billion people. First impressions of Indians can also be mixed: Indians are a blend of the modern and the traditional, and many do not perceive this as a contradiction. As Amaryta Sen, India's Nobel laureate in economics said, "Whatever you can rightly say about India, the opposite is also true" (2005, p. 37). Likewise, a first-time sojourner to the U.S. from India may be struck by some similar impressions of technology, materialism, wastefulness, diversity, homelessness, and space, many of which may run counter to the stereotypical images found in U.S. media. Thus, preparing students for such first impressions can be an important part of predeparture orientations or courses.

In our discussion of this issue, four dimensions of national culture highlighted by Hofstede (2004) have proven useful in determining challenges for cultural adjustment of exchange participants in the respective host country; broadly, these include individualism vs. collectivism, hierarchy, communication styles, and gender relations. In discussing these differences, it is important to remember that there are vast differences within the cultures of both India and the U.S. (urban/rural differences, for example) and that the following reflect general patterns in these cultures reflected in research. Of course, not all individuals fit these patterns, and there are many other cultural differences beyond the ones highlighted below. Because our discussion is organized based on Hofstede's work on Indian culture, it focuses more on the challenges that U.S. students might face in India rather than vice versa

Individualism vs. Collectivism

The cultural dimension of individualism and collectivism is perhaps the one that best highlights the difference between the cultures of the U.S. and India.

According to Hofstede (2004), Indians tend to be more collectivist in their outlook than Americans, meaning they think and act with the group in mind. The concerns of the group, whether the family, the community, or the project team, take precedence over individual choice and preference. This attitude can result in the perception that Indians are less autonomous than Americans and perhaps even less individually responsible. Indians often feel the need to consult with family or friends when making a decision (in the case of Indian students in the U.S., this can mean family consultation on one's major field of study, for example), and "taking advice" from elders is a common practice. Generally speaking, young Indians are more dependent on their families than their American counterparts and accept what could be termed as "interference" from family members in their lives. Children in India are often viewed by Americans as overprotected by their families and not encouraged to do things independently. Arranged marriages are still largely the norm, with parents involved in partner selection. The need to conform to the larger group is felt actively even among the young. Personal matters considered very private in the West are more easily shared in India. For Indian students studying in the U.S., this means that it may be difficult to be on one's own suddenly, especially if this is the first time living apart from parents and family. For instance, in India, students' primary responsibility is to study, while logistics (such as money matters, food, etc.) are taken care of by the parents and family. In the U.S., Indian students not only have to study but are on their own to take care of all other matters, too. Being away from the support network of family can also lead to more loneliness for Indian students, who may be used to having family constantly around them (Thakkar, 2008). On the other hand, an American student in India might find the close proximity of others intrusive when neighbors and friends take a personal interest in the student's life and see this as an invasion of privacy. Further, Indians often collaborate with others on seemingly small projects, and an American student may not be as understanding of such collaboration, given the role of the individual in American culture. For example, an Indian student may actively consult his or her family and friends during the admissions process as well as in the selection of a program of study.

Hierarchy

The issue of hierarchy, or "power distance," as it is also called in some intercultural theories, is compounded by the caste structure in India. The first of four dimensions of national culture elaborated upon by Hofstede is power distance. "The basic issue involved, which different societies handle differently, is human inequality. Inequality can occur in such areas as prestige, wealth and power; different societies put different weights on status consistency among these areas" (2001, p. 79). Status, rank, and age determine who is treated with greater respect and deference than others. There is a clear distinction between classes in India, which influences behavior. Caste traditionally typifies the Indian social structure, which was characterized by hereditary, occupational specialization prior to urbanization and industrialization. These ancient social categories were defined hierarchically and were distinct from each other through stipulations of caste endogamy. Today, caste and class are increasingly divergent, and education and job opportunities have brought greater social mobility.

The faculty-student relationship is hierarchic in India, and this might surprise the American student used to a more egalitarian, informal structure. Traditionally, the teacher in India has commanded great respect, and questioning by students was generally not encouraged, but as the school system has evolved, so has the teacher's power. The American student might find this formal and deferential behavior strange, for in his/her view it does not encourage critical thinking and interactive learning. Also, the form of address commonly used for seniors in India (either "Sir" or "Ma'am") could denote excessive power distance for the American student used to communicating on a more informal basis with others, irrespective of rank and position. Likewise, Indian students in the U.S. may not feel as comfortable in more informal classrooms where students and teachers engage in dialogue and treat each other more informally than in many Indian classrooms.

It is important to note here that the "foreign" person in India is often approached with excessive interest and utmost respect. This attitude is reflected in an Indian saying, "*atithi devo bhava*" (The guest is God).

Intercultural Communication

Intercultural communication is one of the major challenges that students confront, though communicating in India is far easier for native English speakers than in many countries where English is not spoken. Indians tend to be more verbose and indirect when they communicate, which can be interpreted by American students as "not being clear" or "not saying what they mean." "When Indians are being indirect, there is really no equivalent of that in Western culture; when Indians are being direct that equates to Western indirectness; and when Indians are being blunt and on the verge of rude, that's roughly the same as Western directness" (Storti, 2007, p. 64). In a collectivist culture, however, such indirect communication ensures that others' sentiments are respected and relationships preserved, especially within community networks. Disruption of such networks can prove potentially disruptive in a society that is closely interlinked and where contacts matter for marriage alliances, employment opportunities, school admissions, etc. Indirect communication also helps to "save face" but can be extremely confusing to an American for whom a refusal or a criticism is probably just that and nothing more. A frank opinion voiced by an American, for example, particularly about an aspect of Indian culture, could appear rude and disrespectful. Even an honest "I hate spicy food" can be viewed as quite abrupt by Indian hosts.

In India, it is considered discourteous (and contributes to a loss of face) to argue or disagree with seniors, including teachers. "Indians are culturally conditioned not to cause offense and to tell other people what they want to hear, especially superiors and one's elders. What safer way to guarantee harmony and save face, after all, than never to disagree, never to confront" (Storti, 2007, p. 38). Disagreement is generally communicated indirectly. However, for the American student used to a more direct and straightforward form of communication, Indian communication can appear confusing and convoluted. When communicating negative feedback or refusing an invitation, for example, it is important to remember that this is likely to be taken personally and perceived as a rejection of friendship by the Indian host. Thus, Indian exchange participants in the U.S. should resist taking such communication as a personal affront, and all exchange participants should remember the impact of their cultural backgrounds when interacting with others.

In a larger context in India, acknowledging mistakes or admitting that one doesn't know a particular detail related to one's profession or cultural background is tantamount to casting aspersions on one's entire social group. Indians often avoid expressing uncertainty, especially around cultural outsiders, and saving face is crucial to preserving a relationship in India. To that end, it is important for American students to pay close attention to a qualified "yes" answer such as "yes, I think so" or even the absence of "yes" in an Indian response, both of which can indicate a "no." Other techniques of indirect communication used by Indians to communicate disagreement or "no" can include a postponed answer ("let me check and get back to you"), hesitation, or even silence, avoiding the question, or changing the subject (Storti, 2007). On the other hand, Indians may find American directness to be quite blunt, with a disregard for maintaining good relations. Even when asked directly for an opinion, some Indians may not say what they really feel. On the contrary, they might feel offended if an American expresses his or her opinion.

Nonverbal communication can vary as well between the two cultures. For example, American students in India may find difficulty in adjusting to the Indian concept of personal space, given the close proximity often found in India. Nonverbal cues such as head nods in some parts of India can be particularly confusing, since a characteristic shaking of the head in India can mean "yes" and not "no"; Americans often tend to misinterpret this gesture. Other nonverbal gestures that may vary between the two cultures revolve around public displays of affection (more acceptable in the U.S.) and greetings (Kolanad, 2005).

So what do these differences in communication styles mean for administrators of education abroad programs? It is important for these programs to address communication differences directly through predeparture orientation and courses. For example, bring in people who have studied in the U.S. or in India to help students understand what to expect specifically in terms of communication differences. General awareness of communication style differences can greatly aid in alleviating frustrations and culture clashes, even though those will still inevitably occur.

Gender Relations

According to Hofstede's "masculinity index," a concept developed through his analysis of IBM data measuring gender relations and the relative importance attached to "feminine" versus "masculine" work, women are generally treated on a par with men in the U.S., but their status is lower in India, a country where patriarchic sentiment is much higher. Gender relations in India differ from community to community and are governed generally by traditional prescriptions. The relationship between the sexes in many parts of India is not egalitarian, and the male enjoys far more privileges than the female.

Despite this fact, an increasing number of women in India study at the postsecondary level, and they often perform better than the males academically, as frequently cited by Indian media channels and newspaper reports. But despite all this, far more importance is placed on male achievements, which might be disturbing for a society such as the U.S., where women can be more independent and where such independence is largely expected of them. Moreover, women in the U.S. generally do not feel as pressured to conform to traditional social norms as Indian women do.

Having briefly discussed some of the major cultural challenges that students may encounter between the U.S. and India, these challenges lead to the following suggestions when preparing students for Indo-U.S. exchange:

• Go beyond predeparture orientations that focus solely on logistics and general country information. When possible, include more in-depth cultural components and concepts in predeparture activities and materials.

• Specifically address cross-cultural communication differences between the two cultures. Bring in students from both cultures to discuss these further with participants preparing to go abroad.

• When possible, empower students to research more about underlying cultural values and communication styles, as well as to think about how they will respond and adapt to the cultural differences they will encounter.

• Help students move beyond "general ideas" and possible stereotypical thinking. This can be done in numerous ways (including the ones mentioned above), such as having Indian and American students meet together several times, both in pairs and in small groups, to discuss intercultural issues before sojourning abroad.

An Outcome of Indo-U.S. Exchange: Intercultural Competence Development

Numerous research studies often cite intercultural competence development as an outcome of student exchange (Bellamy & Weinberg, 2006; Black, & Duhon, 2006; Gray, Murdock, & Stebbins, 2002; Kitsantas, 2004; Kneebone, 2007; Medina-

Lopez-Portillo, 2004; Williams, 2005; Vande Berg, 2004.). Yet how is intercultural competence defined and from whose perspective? This section briefly explores two models that examine what intercultural competence may "look like" as one outcome of student exchange from the U.S. and Indian perspectives. The discussion includes implications for student exchange and questions for program administrators to consider when designing exchange programs that address students' intercultural competence development.

Getting Along with Others: Intercultural Competence from a U.S. Perspective

Scholars in the U.S. have written on various aspects of this concept for the past five decades (see Spitzberg & Changnon, 2009, for a detailed discussion of various definitions and models of intercultural competence). This concept of intercultural competence has been the focus of numerous conferences and publications in the last several years in countries including the U.S., Germany, and Mexico. Discussions in the U.S. on this topic have placed the concept of intercultural competence largely within the applied contexts of "global workforce development" and "internationalization" efforts at postsecondary institutions. U.S. scholars within various disciplines such as social work, engineering, health care, and education have been researching and working on this concept, often with little interdisciplinary contact. Within the U.S., a variety of terms are currently used to describe essentially the same idea, including global competence, international competence, cross-cultural competence, and global citizenship, to name a few.

What does this concept mean to higher education administrators and intercultural scholars in the U.S.? A national study conducted in the U.S., using a grounded theory approach, was the first to document consensus among leading intercultural scholars in the U.S. on a definition and key elements of this concept (Deardorff, 2006). The consensus definition was broadly defined as "effective and appropriate behavior and communication in intercultural situations." The specific agreed-upon elements were categorized into attitudes, knowledge, skills and internal and external outcomes.

Elements of Intercultural Competence

Attitudes: Based on the 2006 Deardorff study, three key attitudes emerged: respect, openness, and curiosity. Openness and curiosity imply willingness to risk and to move beyond one's comfort zone. In communicating respect to others, it is important to demonstrate that others are valued (although the manifestation of demonstrating respect will, of course, vary by cultural context). This begins through showing interest in others—in their families and their cultures—and in simply listening attentively. These attitudes are foundations for the further development of knowledge and skills needed for intercultural competence.

Given these three foundational attitudes of intercultural competence, the following questions arise in preparing students for international exchange, in this case between India and the U.S.:

- How is respect demonstrated in the host culture? How can students show they value others' beliefs, opinions, and cultural practices even when they may disagree with them?

- How open and curious are students in learning more about the host culture in which they will be living? (For example, what questions do students have about the host culture? Have they researched answers to those questions— from multiple perspectives?)

- Are students quick to make assumptions or judge a situation? If so, how can students be challenged to move beyond assumptions and judgments that impact their attitudes?

Knowledge: In the U.S., there is some debate as to the kinds of "global knowledge" that college graduates need. In the 2006 Deardorff study, intercultural scholars agreed that the following knowledge was necessary for intercultural competence: cultural self-awareness (meaning the ways in which one's culture has influenced one's identity and worldview), culture-specific knowledge, deep cultural knowledge including understanding other world views, and sociolinguistic awareness. Many definitions have been used for the word "culture." For the purposes of this discussion, "culture" is defined as values, beliefs and norms held by a group of people. Culture shapes how individuals communicate and behave; that is, how they interact with others. Culture-specific knowledge refers to specific facts about another culture—correct protocol to be followed when giving a gift, for example. Deep cultural knowledge refers to structural influences on a culture, including history, religion, economics, and other factors. It is important to note that the only element agreed upon by all the intercultural scholars in this study was the importance of understanding the world from others' perspectives.

Given these key components of knowledge necessary for intercultural competence development, exchange programs need to explore the following questions:

- To what degree are students culturally self-aware—before going abroad as well as while they are abroad? Can they describe their own worldview and the impact of cultural conditioning on their own beliefs and values? Can they articulate changes in their cultural self-awareness throughout the experience?

- What specific cultural knowledge do students already possess about the host culture before engaging in the exchange experience? What are some of the gaps in their cultural knowledge and do they know how to obtain such knowledge?

- Are students aware of the underlying cultural frameworks for the host culture, as well as for their own culture (i.e., underlying cultural values, communication styles, and so on) and the impact of this subjective culture on interactions?

- How can students move beyond surface cultural knowledge to understanding more deeply the worldviews of the host culture, especially during the exchange experience?

Skills: The skills that emerged from this study as elements of intercultural competence include different ways of processing knowledge: observing, listening, evaluating, analyzing, interpreting, and relating. These skills also indicate the importance of process, meaning the ways in which these skills are developed, and critical reflection to the overall development of intercultural competence.

These skills lead to the following questions for program administrators:

- How can administrators help students hone their observation, listening, and cognitive skills so that they begin to think interculturally?

- Do students know how to evaluate interactions and situations through an intercultural lens?

- Are students encouraged to engage in active critical reflection of their interactions with host nationals? Are program administrators involved in guiding students through critical reflection on their experience so as to enhance students' intercultural learning while abroad? Do students not only seek to understand why something occurred but also to identify lessons learned?

Internal Outcomes: The attitudes, knowledge, and skills described above ideally encourage students to behave with greater flexibility, adaptability, ethnorelative perspective, and empathy. These are internal outcomes that occur within the individual as a result of the acquired attitudes, knowledge, and skills necessary for intercultural competence. At this point, individuals are able to see from others' perspectives and to respond to them according to the way in which the other person desires to be treated. Individuals may reach this outcome to varying degrees.

These internal outcomes give rise to the following questions for program administrators:

- Do students know how host nationals want to be treated or do students assume host nationals want to be treated by students' own cultural standards?

- Are students able to adapt their behavior and communication style to accommodate those in the host culture?

- Can students view knowledge, cultural artifacts, issues, and situations from multiple perspectives?

External Outcomes: The behavior and communication of the individual ultimately reflect the synthesis of the attitudes, knowledge, skills, and internal outcomes associated with intercultural competence. How effective and appropriate is this person in intercultural situations? Individual behavior and communication are the external outcomes of intercultural competence. The definition of intercultural competence that scholars have agreed upon is thus based on effective and appropriate behavior and communication in intercultural situations. However, it is important to understand that many underlying, complex processes are necessary to produce this observable outcome. It is also important to understand the ways that behavior and communication are determined to be "effective" and "appropriate." Effectiveness can be determined by the interlocutor, but appropriateness can only be determined by the other person, whose cultural norms of appropriateness structure this determination.

Thus, these external outcomes suggest the following questions:

- How culturally appropriate are students in their interactions with host nationals? How would host nationals respond to that question?
- Are students able to meet their goals in an appropriate and effective manner within the host culture context?
- Do students reflect on how they could improve their interactions with host nationals?

These five overall elements can be visualized through the following model of intercultural competence:

FIGURE 7.1: PROCESS MODEL OF INTERCULTURAL COMPETENCE

Individual

Attitudes:
Respect (valuing other cultures); Openness (withholding judgment); Curiosity and discovery (tolerating ambiguity)

Knowledge & Comprehension:
Cultural self-awareness, deep cultural knowledge, sociolinguistic awareness
SKILLS: To listen, observe and evaluate; To analyze, interpret, and relate

Process Orientation

Desired External Outcome:
Effective and appropriate communication and behavior in an intercultural situation

Desired Internal Outcome:
Informed frame of reference shift (adaptability, flexibility, ethnorelative view, empathy)

Interaction

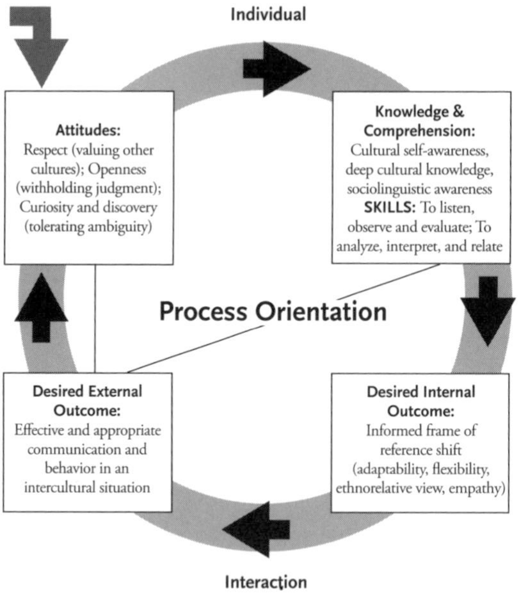

Notes:
· *Begin with attitudes; move from individual level (attitudes) to interaction level (outcomes)*
· *Degree of intercultural competence depends on acquired degree of attitudes, knowledge/comprehension, and skills*

Source: Deardorff, 2006

This model illustrates that it is possible for an individual to have the requisite attitudes and be minimally effective and appropriate in behavior and/or communication, even without further knowledge or skills. Adding the necessary knowledge and skills may ensure that an individual can be more effective and appropriate in his or her interactions. With the added flexibility, adaptability, and empathy, one can be even more effective and appropriate in intercultural interactions. This model also illustrates the importance of an ongoing approach to the development of intercultural competence, which is a life-long journey, as noted by the circular form of the model.

In exploring this consensus-based model of intercultural competence from a U.S. perspective, several observations can be noted. This model is centered around the individual, which means that the knowledge, skills, and attitudes acquired by that individual become the basis for successful intercultural interactions. An emphasis on the individual suggests that this model for understanding intercultural competence development is itself grounded, to some extent, in the privileged place of individualism in U.S. culture. In examining this model further, it is important to observe what is not present in the various aspects of intercultural competence, foremost of those being language. Interestingly enough, the experts in this study could not reach a consensus on the role of language in intercultural competence, which implied that language was a necessary but not sufficient element. In reflecting further upon this model, it is also important to note that specific elements, such as respect, may manifest themselves differently in different cultural contexts.

Having explored a U.S. perspective on intercultural competence, we now turn our attention to an Indian perspective on this concept. This is one model developed from the experience of this chapter's two Indian co-authors in training participants in exchanges between the two cultures, and it cannot be considered the definitive Indian definition of intercultural competence.

India: A Context for Intercultural Competence

Perhaps for the first time in the history of modern India, demand for talent has outstripped its supply. Within the higher education sector, campus recruitment was still a novelty in India a decade ago. The perception that India needs to acquire a "global mindset" has been gaining ground and, as in the U.S., it has been largely situated in the context of "global workforce development."

Having said this, it is important to note that in India, unlike in the U.S., there has not been a perceived need, until recently, to explore the concept of intercultural competence across various disciplines, although this has begun to emerge in the "campus-to-corporate" programs that prepare new recruits for their first jobs in information technology companies. Prior to this, the understanding of this concept was equated simply with knowing a foreign language. Thus, the concept of intercultural competence remains a new area in the higher education sector in India. Today, language knowledge is still prioritized as key to intercultural competence development. Moreover, in the authors' experience, the belief that being in the proximity of another culture equips one with intercultural competence is widely held in India.

IIE/AIFS Foundation Global Education Research Reports
INTERNATIONAL INDIA: A TURNING POINT IN EDUCATIONAL EXCHANGE WITH THE U.S.

87

The need for "effective and appropriate behavior and communication in intercultural situations" (Deardorff, 2006) is being felt as India seeks to maintain its competitive outsourcing advantage. This is being addressed primarily in corporate India through English language training, voice and accent neutralization, presentation skills, and cross-cultural training programs. In fact, "many Indian vendors provide cultural training for their employees, especially for those who are going to the West but also for those who remain in India but who will regularly interact by phone or email with Western colleagues" (Storti, 2007, p.11). Further, "while cultural training is necessary and beneficial, in most cases, it only raises awareness…. Much of so-called cultural training is not in fact cultural, dealing with differences in values and behavior, but 'country' training," with "facts about the target country…" and a "list of dos and don'ts…. The danger in cultural training for Indians is the false sense of security it may give them…." (Storti, 2007, p. 11–12). It is interesting to note that the foreign language institutes in India are now providing cross-cultural training for European companies doing business with India. The NASSCOM-McKinsey report (2005) considers only a fraction of the 2.5 million new graduates that India produces suited for work in a global environment, since many students lack the skills and quality required for the offshore IT and business process outsourcing (BPO) sectors.

As the higher education sector in India globalizes, the need to further develop this concept will be felt more intensely. Interestingly enough, it is Indian students' parents, with a more globalized view of higher education, who are encouraging students to go abroad for studies (Pal, 2008). Even though students from India form the largest contingent from any single country studying in the U.S. (Bhandari & Chow, 2008) and most Indian students come to the U.S. for the perceived professional advantages acquired through U.S. study, Thakkar (2008) found that Indian students surprisingly fail to derive the benefits of intercultural interaction during their educational experiences in the U.S., sometimes displaying a lack of curiosity about the other cultures they encounter. Further, Thakkar found that Indian students in the U.S. place intercultural learning at a much lower priority than educational and career goals. These findings raise several questions that can further be explored by study abroad administrators:

- What are the implications of these priorities for preparedness of Indian students in the U.S. for situations that require intercultural contact and intercultural competence?

- As more and more international students study at Indian institutions of higher education, what challenges will these international students face during their study abroad experience in India (as previously discussed in this chapter)?

- In both cases, what steps can educational programs take to ensure that intercultural learning and the development of students' intercultural competence actually occur?

- What evidence will document the outcomes of these exchange programs?

An Indian Perspective on Intercultural Competence

When discussing intercultural competence from an Indian perspective, it is first important to recognize various influences on an Indian view of intercultural competence, including religious and historical influences. Indian culture is predominantly Hindu but pronouncedly plural, with active Muslim, Christian, and other religious communities that have all been influenced by each other at various stages of the country's history. The concept of "purdah," or veiling, for example, is readily associated with Islam but is also practiced by many Hindu communities in Rajasthan and Gujarat, where it is considered appropriate for women to cover their heads. In fact, the teachings of Buddhism and Hinduism, among other Asian belief systems, dictate a holistic, interconnected worldview (Chen & An, 2009) that allows for some borrowing of elements across faiths.

Given that over 80 percent of the Indian population professes a belief in Hinduism (Kolanad, 2005), it is helpful to explore one model of intercultural competence that is derived from Hindu beliefs. Hinduism propagates a deep sense of the oneness in all, the *Atman* or Self, based on five capsules as summed up by Hindu religious leader Swami Paramarthananda (2002):

1. I am of the nature of eternal and all pervading consciousness.

2. I am the only source of permanent peace, security and happiness.

3. By my mere presence I give life to the body and mind, and through my body and mind I experience the material world outside.

4. Whatever happens in the world, my body and mind, does not affect me, the consciousness.

5. By remembering this fact, I turn life into an entertainment or sport; by forgetting this fact, I turn life into a struggle.

Those who are influenced by such religious beliefs may feel that these beliefs equip adherents to become "cultural chameleons," a commonly used metaphor among those of us who work in the intercultural arena (Pusch, 2009). This ability to become a cultural chameleon has helped many Indians succeed in arenas such as economics, society, or politics, whether in India or abroad. These successful Indians have been able to preserve their own values and identities while adapting to external behaviors in many contexts.

Inclusiveness reflects the Hindu worldview, which is based on cooperation among different segments of a society and which traditionally was nonegalitarian and structured according to caste. Having said this, it is important to point out that globalization is contributing to reducing caste stigmas while reinforcing the "social capital" that caste status conveys. Gurumurthy (2009) argues that caste affiliations help groups to connect and prosper through social networking in a progressively atomized world because of their shared social capital. We assume here that it is this social capital, created through identification with caste, class, and regional and linguistic affinities, which intrinsically anchors Indian students abroad and makes them feel secure and able to adjust. This is somewhat similar to an American leveraging his or her alumni contacts.

Figure 7.2 illustrates one model of intercultural competence based on the influence of Hindu beliefs in Indian society. In viewing this model, it is important to recognize that India is largely a secular country with the active presence of all faiths. Whereas in the West, secular is often used to refer to the opposite of religious, in India it more often refers to the inclusion of all faiths. As Dr. Radhakrishnan, former President of India, writes in *Recovery of Faith* (as cited in Bakshi, 2001), "When India is said to be a secular state, it does not mean that we reject the reality of an unseen spirit or the relevance of religion .... It does not mean that secularism itself becomes a positive religion ... [it means that] we hold that not one religion should be given preferential status...." Thus, readers are encouraged to seek other models of intercultural competence from other Indian perspectives and consider the following as representing one view within many possibilities. For example, another model of intercultural competence based on Indian philosophy (Carpenter & Saxena, 2008) places self-reflection at the core of intercultural competence and discusses Indian philosophical principles related to mindfulness, adaptation, and *maya*, or being aware of one's own lens and how it can hold one back from being successful. At the core of this Hindu-based model is the belief in the oneness of all, of unity within diversity. One may find that a certain "Indianness" prevails, despite the vast diversity with India and its 28 states, and many feel they understand each other through the lens of this core oneness of all. Oneness of all is what both the Indian co-authors have seen while training thousands of Indians in their online workshops; it is a subtle inner belief that in the end makes global Indians resilient and successful in working with each other and with others in the world. In our view, it is almost like a fine cosmic dance of adjustments that goes on because of this thought of oneness in all that prevails in the end.

FIGURE 7.2: INTERCULTURAL COMPETENCE MODEL, INDIAN PERSPECTIVE

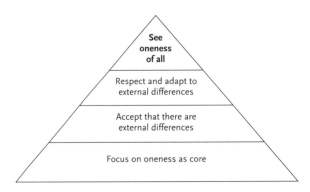

Implications for Student Exchange

As students embark on an exchange program, it is crucial that they prepare themselves as much as possible to understand the worldview of the other culture—by exploring the following questions through such venues as predeparture orientations or courses:

1. What underlying cultural values are important to understand?

2. How do these cultural values influence behaviors that I may encounter in the other culture?

3. What are some of the key influences (philosophical, economic, historical, etc.) on the worldview(s) found in the other culture?

4. What do I know about the worldview(s) in the other culture? Can I analyze intercultural situations through multiple worldviews?

5. How are these multiple worldviews similar or different from each other, and how can I begin to navigate within these different ways of seeing the world?

6. How can I develop my own identity while adapting my external behavior to intercultural situations I will encounter in the other culture?

7. How do I derive meaning from my exchange experience in regard to my own intercultural learning, including the impact of the experience on my own worldview, self-awareness, and identity?

So to sum it up, there is much work yet to be done in regard to intercultural competence from various Indian perspectives. The model presented here suggests that the underlying principle of this concept may be the oneness of all. In an intercultural environment of difference, respect and acceptance of the other—as in the notion of "live and let live"—are posited, resulting in increased inclusiveness and corresponding declines in prejudice and exclusivity. To tie this into Western scholars' work on intercultural competence, Kohls (1994) posits that explicit behavior above the watermark of the iceberg of culture is dictated by the implicit values and beliefs that lie below the surface. To understand Indians' behaviors, then, it is important to understand the underlying values and beliefs that influence this behavior, a few of which were discussed earlier in this chapter.

Comparison of U.S. and Indian Perspectives on Intercultural Competence

On first comparison, many initial differences emerge between these two perspectives on intercultural competence. The U.S. model is rooted firmly in individualism, placing the individual at the core when discussing the attitudes, knowledge, and skills needed for an individual to develop intercultural competence. The Indian model highlighted in this chapter is rooted in relationships, emphasizing the oneness of all at its core. This

Indian model stresses acceptance and adaptation as outcomes of intercultural competence, while the U.S. model focuses on effective and appropriate interactions.

But while the differences between these perspectives on intercultural competence are significant, it is also important to examine the common themes found in both models. Certainly, a common theme of respect runs through both models, although that respect may be manifested differently in each culture. Further, the common themes of understanding others' backgrounds and of having empathy are key to both models. These common themes then lead to adaptability, which is also highlighted in both the U.S. and Indian models of intercultural competence. Examining these common themes further can point to some possible outcomes of Indo-U.S. exchange in that a key outcome of such exchange would be a greater understanding of each others' culture and worldview, which in turn leads to a higher degree of empathy—of truly having a grasp of the other's perspective. This understanding can then lead to a greater degree of adaptability, which is a hallmark of intercultural competence (from multiple perspectives).

Implications of Intercultural Competence Perspectives

Having explored these different perspectives on intercultural competence, what are the practical implications in student exchange? From an Indian perspective, it is important for students to understand difference within the bigger picture of oneness. At a deeper level, students can be challenged to focus on what is core to their own beliefs and identity, as well as to engage in relationship-building from a different perspective. From the U.S. perspective, it is important to focus on the process of intercultural competence development, both in the preparation as well as throughout students' intercultural experiences, and especially after the experience ends, since time spent processing the entire experience is essential to greater intercultural learning and development of intercultural competence. Programs need to ensure that sufficient time is spent with students before they engage in the intercultural experience, for example in the setting of a specific course, so that they gain deeper cultural insights prior to or during the experience abroad. Specifically, *Inside Higher Ed* reported that "several colleges are starting special courses in India for American students to spend an intense month of study, typically preceded or followed by instruction in the United States. Among such courses are a College of St. Catherine course focused on issues of poverty in the lives of Indian women and a Goucher College course that uses study of Indian religions and arts to explore broader themes about the country" (Jaschik, 2006). Sufficient time also needs to be spent after the experience to help students process the intercultural learning that occurred and in so doing to help move students beyond compartmentalizing the experience.

This also means that students are not left to their own devices during their time overseas; rather, continued intervention in students' intercultural learning engages them throughout their experience (Deardorff, 2008). Through interactions and relationships, mutual learning occurs, ideally resulting in increased intercultural competence. A balance of the Indian and U.S. perspectives on intercultural competence will lead to successful interactions between students from both countries as exchange programs between India and the U.S. continue to evolve.

It is important to note that intercultural competence is indeed a lifelong journey. Providing students with the mechanisms and tools to engage in intercultural learning is crucial to their development, so that students have a better understanding of the intercultural concepts involved in the study abroad experience. Such mechanisms include the following:

- Guiding students to a greater cultural self-awareness (reflection is a key part of this process) and the ways in which a student's culture influences his or her identity;

- Providing students with opportunities to hone their intellectual skills to gather cultural information, including deep cultural knowledge (which includes underlying cultural values; communication styles; and historical, social, and religious contexts), and to be able to analyze and apply that information in their daily lives;

- Focusing on knowledge and activities that encourage and challenge students to see from different cultural perspectives (this is where the two different intercultural competence models could be addressed) while at the same time understanding the unity within diversity;

- Facilitating opportunities for students to engage in meaningful and substantive interactions and relationship-building activities with those in the host culture; and

- Ensuring that students are given time for critical reflection on their intercultural learning and experiences during the program and beyond so that they can continue to reflect on their own intercultural learning throughout their lives.

When discussing how the cultures of other lands impact the culture of India, Gandhi said "I do not want my house to be walled in on all sides and my windows to be stuffed. I want the cultures of all the lands to be blown about my house as freely as possible. But I refuse to be blown off my feet by any." This thought illustrates key elements of intercultural competence: open-mindedness, respectfulness, self-awareness, and identity. Student exchange can lead to these outcomes and more. The ultimate goal of intercultural competence—learning to live together—is an essential part of our shared future. And as Dr. Martin Luther King Jr. said, "we must learn to live together as brothers or perish together as fools."

REFERENCES

Bakshi, P.M. (2001). *The Constitution of India*. New Delhi: Universal Law Publishing Co.

Bellamy, C., & Weinberg, A. (2006). Creating global citizens through study abroad. *Connection: The Journal of the New England Board of Higher Education, 21*(2), 20–21.

Bhandari, R., & Chow, P. (2008). *Open doors 2008: Report on international educational exchange*. New York: Institute of International Education.

Black, H.T., & Duhon, D.L. (2006). Assessing the impact of business study abroad programs on cultural awareness and personal development. *Journal of Education for Business, 81*(3), 140–144.

Bok, D. (2006). *Our underachieving colleges: A candid look at how much students learn and why they should be learning more*. Princeton: Princeton University Press.

Carpenter, K., & Saxena, V. (2008, January 19). *Traditional Indian philosophy: A new model of cross-cultural competency*. Presentation given at the 2008 conference of the Society for Intercultural Education Training And Research (SIETAR)-India, Pune, India.

Chen, G., & An, R. (2009). A Chinese model of intercultural leadership competence. In D.K. Deardorff (Ed.), *The SAGE handbook of intercultural competence* (pp. 196–208). Thousand Oaks, CA: Sage.

Deardorff, D.K. (2008). Intercultural competence: A definition, model and implications for education abroad. In V. Savicki (Ed.), *Intercultural competence and transformation: Theory, research, and application*. Sterling, VA: Stylus Publishing.

Deardorff, D.K. (2006). The identification and assessment of intercultural competence as a student outcome of internationalization at institutions of higher education in the United States. *Journal of Studies in International Education*, Fall 2006, 241–266.

Hofstede, G. (2004). *Cultures and organizations: Software of the mind*. New York: McGraw-Hill.

Gray, K.S., Murdock, G.K., & Stebbins, C.D. (2002). Assessing study abroad's effect on an international mission. *Change, 34*(2), 44–52.

Gupta, A.K., & Govindarajan, V. (2002). Cultivating a global mindset. *Academy of Management Executive, 16*(1), 116–126.

Gurumurthy, S. (2009, January 19). Is caste an economic development vehicle? *The Hindu*.

Hofstede, G. (2004). *Cultures and organizations: Software of the mind*. New York: McGraw-Hill.

Hofstede, G. (2001). *Culture's consequences: Comparing values, behaviors, institutions, and organizations across nations*. Thousand Oaks, CA: Sage Publications.

Jaschik, S. (2006, February 1). Passage to India. *Inside Higher Ed*. Retrieved November 9, 2009 from http://www.insidehighered.com/layout/set/dialog/layout/set/print/news/2006/02/01/india.

Kitsantas, A. (2004, September). Studying abroad: The role of college students' goals on the development of cross-cultural skills and global understanding. *College Student Journal*.

Kneebone, T. (2007). Developing cross-cultural awareness and understanding. *Independent School, 67*(1), 80–91.

Knight, J. (2009). New developments and unintended consequences: Wither thou goest, internationalization? In R. Bhandari & S. Laughlin, *Higher education on the move: New developments in global mobility* (pp. 113–123). New York: Institute of International Education.

Kohls, R. (1994). *Intercultural trainers' handbook*. Portland, OR: Summer Institute for Intercultural Communication.

Kolanad, G. (2005). *Culture Shock! India*. Portland, OR: Graphic Arts Center Publishing.

Medina-López-Portillo, A. (2004). Intercultural learning assessment: A link between program duration and the development of intercultural sensitivity. *Frontiers: The Interdisciplinary Journal of Study Abroad, 10*(Fall), 179–199.

NASSCOM-McKinsey. (2005). *NASSCOM-McKinsey report 2005: Extending India's leadership of the global IT and BPO industries*.

Pal, A. (2008, June 19–July 2). 12 Steps to Studying Abroad. *Outlook Money, 7*(13), 22–33.

Paramarthananda. (2002). *Introduction to Vedanta*. Chennai: Shastraprakashika Press Trust.

Pusch, M. (2009). The interculturally competent global leader. In D.K. Deardorff (Ed.), *The SAGE handbook of intercultural competence* (pp. 66–84). Thousand Oaks, CA: Sage.

Sen, A. (2005). *The argumentative Indian: Writings on Indian history, culture, and identity*. New York: Picador.

Spitzberg, B., & Changnon, G. (2009). Conceptualizing intercultural competence. In D.K. Deardorff (Ed.), *The SAGE handbook of intercultural competence* (pp. 2–52). Thousand Oaks, CA: Sage.

Storti, C. (2007). *Speaking of India: Bridging the communication gap when working with Indians*. Boston: Intercultural Press.

Thakkar, R. (2008). [The rhetoric and reality of intercultural contact: A case study of Indian students in the United States]. Unpublished thesis, North Carolina State University, Raleigh, North Carolina.

Vande Berg, M. (Ed.). (2004). Special issue on the assessment of student learning abroad. *Frontiers: The Interdisciplinary Journal of Study Abroad, 10*.

Williams, T.R. (2005). Exploring the impact of study abroad on students' intercultural communication skills: Adaptability and sensitivity. *Journal of Studies in International Education, 9*(4), 356–371.

Chapter Eight
CREATING INDO-U.S. HIGHER EDUCATION PARTNERSHIPS: LESSONS LEARNED AT THE UNIVERSITY OF CALIFORNIA, DAVIS

NICOLE RANGANATH, DIRECTOR, INTERNATIONAL & OUTREACH INITIATIVES,
UNIVERSITY OF CALIFORNIA, DAVIS

India's importance for U.S. higher education is longstanding and has steadily increased since World War II. With the postwar liberalization of U.S. immigration law, especially after the Immigration and Nationality Act of 1965, India became a crucial sending country for U.S. universities in search of highly qualified students. The late 1960s ushered in the era of so-called brain drain, in which science and engineering students from the best Indian technical institutes, the Indian Institute of Science and the Indian Institutes of Technology, earned their PhDs from leading U.S. universities (Ruggiero, 2006; Takaki, 1989). Many of those who made up this wave of Indian students remained in the U.S. to become influential scientists, academics, and entrepreneurs. In the 2001/02 academic year, India became the top sending country for international students in the U.S. (Koh Chin, 2002). Recently there has also been strong growth in the number of U.S. college students interested in studying in India. In fact, India recently entered the list of the top 20 host countries for U.S. college students studying abroad.

The University of California, Davis' linkages to India emerged from its tradition as a land grant institution with deep roots in agriculture. Founded in 1909, University of California, Davis (UC Davis) began as the University Farm School, and it continues to be the leading institution for agricultural and veterinary medical research in the state. UC Davis is still best known for its agricultural and environmental science programs 50 years after it became a comprehensive university in 1959. UC Davis is one of the 10 campuses of the University of California. It is a tier-one research university and ranks 11th among U.S. public universities in research funding. The university is considered a leader in interdisciplinary research and study in areas including agriculture, health, energy, and the environment.

For over 50 years, UC Davis faculty researchers have helped to promote development in India by increasing food production, alleviating poverty, and stimulating economic development. As early as the 1930s, the research of UC Davis agricultural engineers and plant scientists led to increased rice production. Gurdev Khush, one of the world's leading plant scientists, is recognized as one of the fathers of the green revolution in rice production. Dr. Khush, a UC Davis alumnus and a native of Punjab, India, led the breeding program at the International Rice Research Institute (IRRI) in the Philippines. He is credited with ushering in the green revolution in global rice production with the release of the variety "IR36," the most widely planted rice variety ever grown. Now an adjunct professor at UC Davis, Khush and other researchers are working today to develop hardier rice varieties that can better withstand harsh environmental factors and pests. He won the World Food Prize in 1996 and is credited with saving millions of lives in India and throughout the developing world (Stumbos, 2009).

Today UC Davis pursues research and educational collaborations in a wide range of disciplines in India. Formal partner relationships with Indian institutions are still primarily in agriculture, and there have been significant capacity-building projects in agriculture and food science. There are also active research collaborations with UC Davis faculty in engineering, energy, medicine, neuroscience, primate research, and many other disciplines. UC Davis recently established the Middle East/South Asia Studies Program and created a Hindi/Urdu language program with support from the U.S. Department of Education.

The Broader Context: Creating Systemwide University of California-India Partnerships

UC Davis' India linkages are part of the broader capacity and formal partnerships in the University of California (UC) system. The University of California launched an ambitious initiative to create large-scale interdisciplinary collaborations with Indian partners in 2005. India was identified as one of the four priority countries (the other three are China, Mexico, and Canada) for research collaborations by UC's Office of the President under Robert Dynes, the former president, and Gretchen Kalonji, director, international strategy development. The purpose of the UC-India Initiative is to harness the collective strengths of the ten UC campuses, together with leading Indian academic, private, and government partners, to provide solutions to shared challenges facing the people of California and India. Indian partners include the Department of Science and Technology (DST), the largest funding agency of the Government of India across many disciplines and institutions; the Department of Biotechnology; and the Indo-U.S. Science and Technology Forum, an autonomous, bilateral, nongovernmental agency designed to promote and catalyze Indo-U.S. bilateral collaborations in science and technology. Indian institutional partners included the Indian Institute of Technology in Kanpur, the Indian Institute of Science in Bangalore, the Jawaharlal Nehru Center for Advanced Scientific Research, and Amrita University in Tamil Nadu (Kalonji, 2005).

The key hallmarks of the UC-India Initiative are:

1. To create an ambitious research initiative involving large-scale inter-disciplinary collaborations that are based on a broad partnership between science, technology, and economic development;

2. To create innovative models for research focused on "common challenges facing India and California with curriculum development and faculty and student exchange"; and

3. To translate joint research to practical benefits for communities in California and India.

The first specific initiative focused on improving engineering education in India, which has been in decline for years. The University of California, together with Carnegie Mellon, Cornell University, the State University of New York at Buffalo, Case Western Reserve University, and bilateral industry partners, joined Amrita University in Tamil Nadu to enhance science and engineering education in India via a new satellite e-learning network. The partnership launched Edusat, a satellite that transmits educational programming to multiple universities across India. As Gretchen Kalonji stated, "By expanding opportunities for international academic collaborations in critical fields, this partnership will not only help keep the University of California competitive, but it will help drive global innovation and economic prosperity."

Unfortunately, the future of this initiative is uncertain due to budgetary constraints in California, not India. Just as the partners agreed to provide bilateral funding for a seed grant program in critical areas of joint research, the downturn in the California economy occurred in 2008. For the foreseeable future, it appears that joint research will be driven primarily by faculty at the ten University of California campuses with their colleagues in India.

Forging Campus-wide India Linkages: The Role of the International Programs Office

In 1999, the Office of University Outreach and International Programs (UOIP) was created to provide greater visibility and coordination in advancing the internationalization efforts of UC Davis. Of all of the international offices at the ten University of California campuses, UOIP is led by the most senior administrator, Vice Provost Bill Lacy, and it is one of the only international offices in the UC system that is part of the offices of the chancellor and provost.

At UC Davis, the international office's approach to advancing international research and education is shaped by the following guiding principles. First, internationalization is central to the mission of UC Davis. Second, UOIP offers a highly integrated approach to internationalizing the university by supporting international research initiatives in addition to international student and scholar mobility programs. Third, internationalization is best achieved by faculty-to-faculty collaborations. Fourth, international offices can play a vital role in advancing the internationalization of the university by offering a wide range of resources to facilitate faculty-led collaborations in the academic departments and programs across the university.

The Growth of International Activity at UC Davis

UC Davis is a global campus that is deeply committed to international education. As of 2007/08, UC Davis ranked fourth of all U.S. universities in hosting international scholars, with 2,543 (Bhandari & Chow, 2008). UC Davis has more than 5,800 international alumni from 131 countries, and the university has a significant undergraduate exchange program with top-tier universities worldwide. The number of UC Davis students participating in study abroad has tripled since 2000, and UC Davis students currently can participate in a broad range of global study and internship experiences through the UC Education Abroad Program and in short-term UC Davis study abroad programs. International students and scholars also enroll in distance education courses and certificate programs offered by UC Davis Extension, the continuing and professional education arm of the university, in a wide array of subjects including viticulture and food science.

India is clearly an important country in UC Davis' international programs. India ranks fourth among sending countries at UC Davis in both the international scholar and international student categories. Nearly half of the scholars conduct research in the College of Agricultural and Environmental Sciences, although significant numbers are attracted by the programs in engineering, the biological sciences, and medicine. It should be noted that UC Davis does not follow the national pattern, which ranks India as the top sending country for students. Instead, China leads the way in sending international students and scholars to UC Davis by a factor of five.

FIGURE 8.1: INTERNATIONAL DEGREE-SEEKING STUDENTS AT UC DAVIS BY PLACE OF ORIGIN, FALL 2008

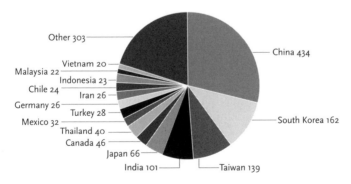

Other 303
Vietnam 20
Malaysia 22
Indonesia 23
Chile 24
Iran 26
Germany 26
Turkey 28
Mexico 32
Thailand 40
Canada 46
Japan 66
India 101
Taiwan 139
China 434
South Korea 162

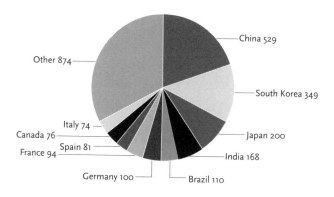

China 529
Other 874
South Korea 349
Italy 74
Canada 76
Japan 200
France 94 Spain 81
India 168
Germany 100
Brazil 110

UC Davis students participating in outbound study abroad programs can study at the University of Delhi and the University of Hyderabad in the University of California Education Abroad Program (EAP) as exchange students on a reciprocal-fee basis. Participation in the EAP in India is modest. In 2008/09, 45 out of the approximately 200,000 students in the UC system studied in the EAP Program in India. There is a proposal at UC Davis to launch a campus-based Summer Abroad Program in Hindustani Music, with the Indian Institute of Technology in Mumbai acting as host institution. In addition, the UC Davis School of Law plans to initiate faculty and student exchange programs with the National Law School of India University in Bangalore. The effort is led by Dr. Beth Greenwood, director of international programs at the School of Law, and interested faculty researchers in corporate, environmental, and human rights law.

The vast majority of international collaborations at UC Davis occur in a decentralized fashion involving direct faculty-to-faculty linkages. However, UOIP has helped to foster research and educational collaborations with India and other countries in the following ways: coordination, communication, faculty resources, and the Seed Grants for International and Outreach Activities Program.

Coordination

UOIP provides campus-wide coordination for international programs, which is a major undertaking in a large public university with four colleges, six professional schools, 31,000 students, 1,500 tenure-track faculty, and over 3,000 adjunct faculty, researchers, and lecturers. The office reviews and formalizes partnership agreements, plans the chancellor's overseas delegations, hosts visiting international delegations, and mobilizes international alumni networks. The office routinely helps to foster new program development and research initiatives by coordinating meetings with faculty and administrators across the university with visiting delegations. In organizing the chancellor's overseas delegations, UOIP builds and sustains relationships with benchmark universities, international alumni, government agencies, and the private sector. Vice Provost Lacy also hired two Asian specialists to help coordinate campus-wide efforts in two key strategic countries—China and India.

Communication

Another key function of the UOIP office is communication, including 1) sharing information about international developments and opportunities with UC Davis faculty and departments, and 2) raising the global profile of UC Davis. The office's critical role in communication was highlighted in the wake of the 2005 tsunami in South and South East Asia. Within a day of the tsunami and the enormous loss of life that followed in its wake, the office formed a campus task force to share the latest information with the university community and to help coordinate media interviews with faculty experts who shared their expertise on South and South East Asia.

The office of UOIP also created a UC Davis Faculty with International Expertise Database to streamline access to information about the international research and educational ties of its faculty members. The database has proven to be a valuable tool for the rapid dissemination of global funding opportunities. Several colleges and schools on campus have tailored the database to include subfields of expertise that are meaningful within their disciplines. The database is also helpful for prospective graduate students, both domestic and international, who are interested in the global expertise and collaborations of their future advisers. Finally, this information is accessible from anywhere in the world, a feature that is appreciated by overseas universities, alumni, and prospective students. The database was highly useful for UC's international initiatives, including India initiatives, and it provided the only efficient mechanism for learning about the many faculty linkages in each country (more information is available at http://uoip.ucdavis.edu/internationalfaculty).

The vice provost and India coordinator have also helped to raise UC Davis' profile in publications, conferences, and government initiatives. UC Davis' leadership role in agricultural development in India is highlighted in the publication, *Ernst & Young-EDGE 2008 Report on Globalizing Higher Education in India* (Palnitkar, 2008, p. 67). The vice provost chaired a bilateral panel session with Indian and U.S. government officials and academics on forging sustainable Indo-U.S. higher education partnerships at the 2007 Annual Conference of the Association of International Education Administrators.

In 2007, UOIP coordinated UC Davis' participation in an effort to attract Indian students to U.S. institutions of higher education. UC Davis was selected among a dozen U.S. universities nationwide to showcase visiting Indian students' testimonials about their experiences in undergraduate and graduate programs. This joint initiative, sponsored by the U.S. Departments of Commerce and State, resulted in videos that were broadcast via public television and the Internet to over 47 million viewers

| Chapter Eight | Nicole Ranganath
CREATING INDO-U.S. HIGHER EDUCATION PARTNERSHIPS: LESSONS LEARNED AT THE UNIVERSITY OF CALIFORNIA, DAVIS

throughout India. UC Davis is hopeful that its participation in this initiative will boost Indian student enrollments in graduate and undergraduate programs. Of the 94,563 Indian students who studied at U.S. universities in the 2007/08 academic year, only 101 studied at UC Davis (Bhandari & Chow, 2008). It is reasonable to expect that the number of visiting Indian students at UC Davis will double within the next few years due in part to this initiative.

Faculty Resources

UOIP has also played a role in sharing information about international funding and grant opportunities with UC Davis faculty. The office created and maintained a comprehensive website featuring international funding opportunities. UOIP also invites senior program officers and government officials to campus to hold workshops about major international funding programs. In addition, the office maintains an email listserv of over 800 faculty to inform them about international funding (more information is available at http://uoip.ucdavis.edu/facultyresources).

UOIP Seed Grants for Outreach and International Activities Program

The UC Davis Seed Grants for Outreach and International Activities program began in 2001 to fund new ideas in outreach and international programs. To date, the Office of University Outreach and International Programs, with matching support from deans, has funded 118 projects with over $1 million, and this seed funding has generated $19 million in external funding. The program has launched innovative educational and research programs in every college and school across the university. The successful projects involved collaborations in 48 countries. Reflecting UC Davis' strong ties to Asia, one-quarter of the projects involved countries in the region, including China, Vietnam, India, Japan, and Taiwan. The program is a cost-effective means of fulfilling the university's mission in engagement and global education—two areas that are critical to UC Davis' tradition as a land grant institution.

The seed grant program has helped to launch a number of India programs over the last eight years. Travis Lybbert, assistant professor in agricultural and resource economics, designed an innovative pocket PC-based mobile lab for field experiments to promote economic development in South India. The seed grant enabled Lybbert to visit Tamil Nadu Agricultural University to disseminate his curriculum development idea to the vice chancellor, faculty, and students. Promising follow-up research projects also emerged, focusing on a new microeconomics course and community outreach with Indian farmers and consumers in food safety. A seed grant helped Randi Hagerman, professor of pediatrics and medical director of the UC Davis MIND Institute, expand her research on the screening and testing of Fragile X Syndrome in India. Fragile X Syndrome is the most common inherited cause of intellectual disability and the most common identifiable cause of autism. Hagerman has established a research partnership with the National Institute of Mental Health and Neuro Sciences (NIMHANS) and leading hospitals in Bangalore to study the prevalence of Fragile X

Syndrome in India and enhanced treatment methods for patients. A third seed grant helped Margaret Swain, senior lecturer in anthropology and women's studies, to establish a new internship program for UC Davis students to intern at IndCare, a non-profit organization in India that helps women achieve greater economic independence.

New Language and Area Studies Programs

One of the key emergent academic programs involving India at UC Davis is the Middle East/South Asia Studies (ME/SA) Program. Professor Suad Joseph, the founding director, started a modest research cluster in 2002 involving faculty and graduate students who studied the Middle East and/or South Asia. At this time, there were only two scholars at UC Davis focusing on these critical geographical regions—a Middle East anthropologist, Suad Joseph, and a South Asian historian, Barbara Metcalf. Five years later, the major in Middle East/South Asia studies had been approved, 19 faculty members were affiliated with the program, 19 new courses had been introduced, and the Arabic and Hindi/Urdu language programs had been created. With the introduction of these two new language programs, the number of non-European languages offered at UC Davis doubled.

At least three key factors enabled the growth of the ME/SA Program within the span of five years. First, the program benefited from the support and advocacy of UC Davis students. Over 800 students signed a petition to launch a major focusing on the Middle East and South Asia, including Arabic and Hindi/Urdu language programs. Second, the founding director and core faculty built the curriculum and provided the vision necessary to draw funding. Third, in 2006 the director successfully obtained a three-year critical funding grant from the U.S. Department of Education's Undergraduate International Studies and Foreign Language Program (UISFL). The university, especially the dean of the Division of Social Sciences, provided cost sharing and made a commitment to support the ME/SA Program, especially the two language programs, after the conclusion of the UISFL grant. The director also cultivated close relationships with heritage communities in the Sacramento region, some of which have led to private donations.

The UOIP office also supported the program during its early stages. The office convened the heads of the various area studies programs in 2004 to reach a consensus about the geographical region that would receive priority in the UISFL proposal. All of the faculty directors agreed that the Middle East and South Asia regions would be the most competitive for government funding in the immediate post-9/11 period. The international office also obtained a grant from the U.S. Department of State Foreign Language Teaching Assistant (FLTA) program. Each year, FLTA allows the university to host two teaching assistants in the Arabic and Hindi/Urdu language programs. The program has helped provide UC Davis students with the opportunity to learn from native speakers and has defrayed language program expenses. Additional funding to establish faculty and graduate student exchange programs linking UC Davis to the Middle East and South Asia was obtained through the UOIP seed grant program.

The future of the ME/SA Program is promising. The new director continues efforts to partner with additional universities abroad. Fundraising efforts are underway to establish programs in additional languages, such as Persian and Tamil. If a third Middle Eastern or South Asian language is offered at UC Davis at the advanced level, then the university will be eligible to apply for more substantial funding through the U.S. Department of Education's National Resource Centers (NRC) program in the near future.

Sustaining UC Davis-India Agricultural Development Programs

UC Davis' global agricultural development projects are primarily coordinated by the College of Agricultural & Environmental Sciences, particularly its International Programs Office, and faculty in over a dozen academic departments. The office has received external funding for development projects in many countries, especially Afghanistan, and projects in Iraq, Egypt, and Jordan have focused on agricultural development and creating postsecondary agriculture curricula. Sustainable large-scale development efforts have been constrained by the long-term decline in U.S. government funding for agricultural development projects. Fortunately, the recent recognition that agriculture is the backbone of developing economies has led to a renewed interest in funding agricultural development projects (J. Hill, personal communication, September 2009).

In India, UC Davis is still best known for excellence in agriculture and large-scale global capacity-building projects in India during the period of plentiful USAID funding in the 1960s and 1970s. The majority of the university's formal partner agreements in India are with agricultural universities. The following is a small sample of recent capacity-building projects with Indian agricultural universities.

Center for Food Quality and Safety at Tamil Nadu Agricultural University

In 2004, UC Davis garnered USAID Higher Education for Development funding to establish a Center for Food Quality and Safety at one of the leading agricultural universities in India, Tamil Nadu Agricultural University (TNAU). This program enabled exchanges between the two universities so that faculty could participate in three annual conferences, and allowed UC Davis scientists to train Indian faculty in techniques and tools designed to reduce post-harvest losses. Beyond the university, the program helped to improve economic national and regional development by disseminating information and technologies designed to reduce the high rate of post-harvest food waste in India to farmers, consumers, and educators. Over a dozen faculty at UC Davis and TNAU participated in the faculty exchange program and annual conferences during the three-year grant period. This program led to substantial changes in

India's national regulations on food safety (J. Hill, personal communication, September 2009). The faculty exchange program paused after the conclusion of the USAID grant, but informal collaborations between the two universities continue (Gore & Odell, 2009).

U.S.-India Agriculture Knowledge Initiative (AKI)

The U.S.-India Agricultural Knowledge Initiative was jointly established in 2005 by the U.S. and Indian governments, together with U.S. land grant universities and Indian universities, the Indian Council for Agricultural Research (ICAR), and private-sector partners. In January 2007, UC Davis faculty participated in a joint workshop on curriculum development in agriculture and rural development. In total, there were 60 participants from leading Indian agricultural universities and 10 U.S. land grant universities, including UC Davis. The workshop subgroups focused on the following topics: enhancing student capacity for rural engagement; partnering with industry for learning, educational technology, and teaching methods; faculty development and continuing education; natural resource and environmental management; and food and health (Sharma, 2007).

Substantial funding from the U.S. government for AKI did not materialize. However, U.S. government allocations were available to support other international scholar programs, including the U.S. Department of State's Hubert H. Humphrey Fellowship Program and the Fulbright Scholar Program. UC Davis is one of 15 U.S. universities to host the prestigious Hubert H. Humphrey Program, which brings accomplished mid-career professionals from the developing world to U.S. universities for leadership training and practical professional growth. With AKI, agricultural development and agricultural economics became the top priority fields in the Humphrey program. At UC Davis, there has been an increase in the number of Humphrey fellows from India (recently 2 to 3 out of the 10 Humphrey fellows hosted each year have been from India). UC Davis also hosts substantial numbers of Fulbright scholars from India, some of whom were supported because agriculture was prioritized.

UOIP supports these agricultural development initiatives in India by providing seed grant funding; administering international scholar programs; and sharing information about funding, faculty ties to India, and other international collaborations.

Lessons Learned and Opportunities

On the basis of the long history of University of California and UC Davis initiatives in India, we can draw various lessons about how to develop sustainable partnerships between U.S. and Indian higher education institutions. Generally, it has been more challenging to sustain campus partnerships with India than with China; coordination, communication, and lack of stable funding streams all pose considerable challenges to maintaining Indo-U.S. higher education collaborations. The most successful initiatives are driven by faculty and students at the university level. However, these grassroots initiatives are more likely to be sustainable if there is also strong support from the administration. Indo-U.S. linkages are also enhanced by programs that involve diverse funding streams and programs positioned to take advantage of long-term commitments and funds at the partnering institutions.

India will continue to figure prominently in UC Davis' internationalization strategy. Chancellor Linda Katehi is strongly committed to increasing the number of international students at UC Davis, and India will be one of the primary sending countries. There are increasing numbers of prominent UC Davis alumni in India who are building multidisciplinary collaborations with leading institutions of higher education, government partners, and the private sector on a campus-wide basis. Promising future possibilities include establishing real-time and asynchronous educational collaborations with the benchmark institutions, and creating joint and dual degree programs between UC Davis and leading Indian higher education institutions. UC Davis will have a wealth of institutional connections and good will from which to draw as the university expands its educational partnerships with India, whether through faculty and student mobility programs, research collaborations, or innovative new partnerships.

REFERENCES

Bhandari, R., & Chow, P. (2008). *Open doors 2008: Report on international educational exchange*. New York: Institute of International Education.

Gore, J.S., & Odell, M.J. (2009, August). Lessons learned from reviews of higher education partnerships in South Asia: An impact assessment of 15 higher education partnerships, 17. Retrieved from http://www.hedprogram.org/Portals/0/PDFs/South%20Asia%20Impact%20Report.8.09.pdf.

Kalonji, G. (2005). The University of California-India Initiative: A partnership for science, technology, and economic development. Davis, CA: University of California Office of the President.

Koh Chin, H.-K. (2002). *Open doors 2002: Report on international educational exchange*. New York: Institute of International Education.

Palnitkar, U. (Ed.). (2008). *Globalizing higher education in India (Ernst & Young-EDGE 2008 report)*. Kolkata and Bangalore: Ernst & Young.

President of India launches historic Indo-U.S. university network. (2005, December 20). *Calit2 Press Releases*. Retrieved from http://www.calit2.net/newsroom/release.php?id=768#

Ruggiero, A. (Ed.). (2006). *The East Indians*. Detroit: Greenhaven Press/Thomson Gale.

Sharma, D.C. (2007, March/April). Preparing for new challenges. *SPAN*, 30-34. Retrieved from http://span.state.gov/wwwhspmarapr0730.html

Stumbos, J. (2009, Spring/Summer). Growing global: How our international programs are taking root. *CA&ES Outlook*, 24. Retrieved from http://ip.ucdavis.edu/docs/outlook-spring09.pdf

Takaki, R. (1989). *Strangers from a different shore: A history of Asian Americans*. New York: Penguin Books.

Chapter Nine

U.S.-India Collaboration in Engineering Education: Prospects for Change under New Leadership?

An Interview with Krishna Vedula, Professor and Dean Emeritus, University of Massachusetts Lowell

IIE: What are your institution's current linkages with institutions in India?

Krishna Vedula: In 2007, University of Massachusetts Lowell (Umass Lowell) founded the Indo-US Collaboration for Engineering Education (IUCEE). This has resulted in active linkages with over 200 engineering colleges in India, including most of the National Institutes of Technology (NITs) and many private and second-tier colleges.

The concept of IUCEE was created in 2007 by over 150 U.S. and Indian leaders of engineering education and businesses. The vision was and is to improve the quality and global relevance of engineering research and education in India by implementing global best practices from the U.S. with the help of the best faculty members. The initial emphasis is on building capacity to improve the teaching quality of faculty in the large number of engineering colleges by introducing the state-of-the-art concepts of problem-based and outcomes-based approaches to teaching and learning. Simultaneously, the resulting networks and collaborations between the U.S. and Indian institutions and faculty are enhancing the culture of research among these colleges. This increases the capacity of the Indian institutions to engage in world-class research addressing crucial problems facing India and the world.

This process has already gotten under way during the past two years. Two philanthropic "IITian" families (alumni of the Indian Institutes of Technology) helped launch the program successfully with more than Rs. 8 crores (US$1.6 million). They included one U.S. family (Deshpande) and one Indian family (Narayana Murthy), along with Infosys Technologies (CEO and IITian Gopalakrishnan). The process is facilitated by Pan IIT, the alumni organization for all Indian Institutes of Technology, in partnership with the American Society for Engineering Education (ASEE), Indian Society for Technological Education (ISTE), and UMass Lowell.

Although the work of IUCEE has only recently begun, the real results of the efforts on the ground and the enormous momentum that the IUCEE has generated make us believe that we are on the right path and give us hope that dramatic results can be achieved in a reasonable time period.

IIE: Now that Kapil Sibal has been appointed as Union Minister for Human Resources Development, what new opportunities do you see for your institution's international activities in India?

KV: During the past two years, IUCEE has tried to engage the Ministry of Human Resources Development (MHRD) and All India Council for Technical Education (AICTE) in the process of large-scale development of engineering faculty in India for the mutual benefit of India and the United States. However, there was little response by the Government of India to the enormous amount of work of IUCEE in India over this time period. With the new leadership under Kapil Sibal, the hope is that this will change. Initial meetings with Kapil Sibal by IUCEE board members, including myself, have been encouraging. But these discussions need to result in action. If a significant change is to happen, the results demonstrated by IUCEE over the past two years need to be supported by the MHRD on a large scale. This should include funding for Indian faculty to conduct and participate in workshops based on the IUCEE model, as well as support for Indian academics traveling to the U.S. to participate in the proposed IUCEE model for research and PhD collaborations.

IIE: What past regulations have complicated your efforts to establish activities in India, and do you think these are likely to change under the new leadership? What reforms to Indian higher education would be ideal from the perspective of your institution?

KV: The major barriers that have complicated the efforts of IUCEE so far have been internal to the Indian engineering education system. These could be streamlined to permit further collaboration in the following ways:

• Developing an effective process for monitoring and accrediting the quality of the engineering institutions (IUCEE has offered to help guide this process along the lines of the U.S. Accreditation Board for Engineering and Technology [ABET] system);

• Granting autonomy to more newly formed private colleges, after a few years of mentoring, so that curricula can respond to the changing needs of society;

• Making a large-scale financial investment to dramatically increase the number of engineering PhDs along the model proposed by IUCEE; and

• Increasing the salary structure for engineering faculty in order to attract and retain the best talent for teaching in this global competitive environment.

These may change under the new leadership. However, many vested bureaucratic interests could thwart this change. Only time will tell if the Indian leadership has the ability and the will to accomplish these changes.

IIE: Do you see a role for U.S. institutions to play in sharing best practices with Indian college leaders, and has your institution pursued work in this area?

KV: This is exactly what UMass Lowell is doing through IUCEE. Over the past two years, IUCEE has been sharing best practices in teaching and research in engineering education through its work with over 25 U.S. engineering colleges and over 200 Indian engineering colleges.

Each year, U.S. experts from prominent U.S. engineering colleges are recruited by IUCEE and UMass Lowell to go to India. These U.S. experts meet with Indian faculty leaders from IITs, NITs, and other top public and private colleges to attend one-week workshops at Faculty Leadership Institutes (FLIs), where they discuss global best practices in teaching and research in their fields. Select Indian faculty leaders then conduct regional workshops on these topics for faculty in second- and third-tier colleges all over India. During the 2008 and 2009 leadership institutes, both conducted at the Infosys Technologies Global Education Centre, 36 professors from the U.S. and 10 industry experts gave 46 workshops to about 585 and 580 faculty members, respectively.

As a follow-up, during 2008 and 2009, Indian faculty members who had participated in the 2008 leadership institute conducted roughly 100 regional workshops, directly impacting more than 3,000 other faculty and 30,000 students. These faculty members used videotapes and other course materials from U.S. experts. Many others have been impacted indirectly by the FLIs through the resulting curriculum revisions at universities and colleges. UMass Lowell and IUCEE have set up 15 IUCEE Regional Centers all over India to coordinate these follow-up efforts. Partnerships have been built with various agencies that are already engaged in similar efforts, such as the National Program on Technology Enhanced Learning (NPTel) through the IITs and the faculty development scheme of the MHRD through the NITs, in order to leverage available resources and expertise. Significant positive outcomes have been demonstrated at over 200 colleges all over India. Researchers have documented amazing results of the radical curriculum revisions implemented by participants in the 2008 FLI, including dramatic improvements in both faculty engagement and student motivation.

UMass Lowell and IUCEE propose to scale up the "Facilitate the Trainer" model for Indian Engineering Faculty Development with ambitious targets. Within the next five years, the goal is to cover all courses in all engineering disciplines and conduct over 2,000 regional workshops reaching over 60,000 engineering faculty in institutions all over India. IUCEE proposes to seek government assistance as well as private support in order to make this model a true public-private partnership.

As a result of improved teaching quality, networks have been created between Indian and U.S. faculty and institutions that have already resulted in research collaborations wherein Indian faculty seeking PhD degrees have found co-guides among U.S. faculty. The second "pillar of research excellence" is being launched in the form of an IUCEE Co-Guide PhD program this year. Indian faculty will be able to obtain high-quality PhDs over four years with the help of distinguished U.S. faculty co-guides. Resulting research collaborations between Indian and U.S. faculty, enabled by faculty exchanges and distance education technologies, will allow large-scale PhD production and research productivity within the next 10 years.

Both countries and the world will benefit as the program develops talent to address the engineering challenges facing the world.

IIE: The issue of how Indian "affirmative action" (the reservation system) will affect future collaboration has figured prominently in recent press discussions of U.S.-India partnerships. Is this likely to be a significant factor in the future activities of your institution in India?

KV: This will have no direct impact on what UMass Lowell or IUCEE does in India.

IIE: The Indian approach to forming international partnerships has been described as decentralized, with each institution setting its own priorities and approaches. The situation in the U.S. is similar. How does this impact efforts to form U.S.-India academic partnerships?

KV: The decentralized nature of both Indian and U.S. engineering education makes the situation ideal for nurturing productive partnerships. The IUCEE approach facilitates this process. The Faculty Leadership Institutes have already built networks for teaching and research collaborations between large numbers of U.S. and Indian faculty and colleges. IUCEE hopes to facilitate this process along the lines of the "shaadi.com" approach [Shaadi.com is an Indian matchmaking website that bills itself as "the world's largest matrimonial service"], wherein individuals and institutions in the U.S. and India publicize their interests and needs through an electronic portal, and partnerships are nurtured through various communication processes facilitated by IUCEE. This is a very positive indicator of potential collaborations between the U.S., the world's most advanced democracy, and India, the world's largest democracy. IUCEE plans to proceed in this direction with help from UMass Lowell.

Concluding Essay

A RETROSPECTIVE LOOK AT INDO-U.S. HIGHER EDUCATION RELATIONS

P.J. LAVAKARE, MEMBER, BOARD OF MANAGEMENT,
SYMBIOSIS INTERNATIONAL UNIVERSITY, PUNE

The year 2009 saw the emergence of two new democratically elected administrations in India and the United States. Both governments are keen to strengthen the relationships between the two countries in various areas of human endeavor—political, economic, and social. Delegations of the two countries have already taken initiatives and have begun to develop strategies for cooperation. The governments of both countries have recognized education—and particularly higher education—as an area of priority for strengthening bilateral relations.

On June 11, 2009, India and the U.S. agreed to set up a joint working group in education headed by the Indian Union Minister for Human Resource Development (the Indian equivalent of a minister of education) and his counterpart in the United States. The U.S. Department of State Bureau of Educational and Cultural Affairs (ECA) is setting up a higher education council to facilitate greater industrial-academic collaboration in educational projects. U.S. Secretary of State Hillary Clinton, in her visit to India, has already promised a "new version" of collaboration with India (Indo-Asian News Service, 2009). All these new initiatives point to a new era in Indo-U.S. higher education relations. Higher education has been an area of common interest to the two countries for the past several decades. However, with the rise of globalization and the knowledge economy, the pursuit of cooperation in higher education is likely to attract even greater attention and to exert an influence on socioeconomic cooperation between India and the U.S.

In the light of these global and bilateral developments, this essay takes a retrospective look at past higher education relations between the two countries in order to shed light on future opportunities and challenges that are likely to emerge in the coming decade. In fact, enhanced and expanded Indo-U.S. higher education relations could be a key factor in developing a long-term partnership between these two large democracies.

Higher Education Relations Between India and the United States—Some Key Issues

Higher education has always been an endeavor that encourages students and scholars to cross national boundaries in search of new knowledge, cutting across cultural barriers and exploring nature and human society. Higher education has also been effective in promoting mutual understanding between nations through exchange of students and scholars working together on challenging problems of mutual interest.

Foreign scholars have traditionally come to India to pursue an understanding of its rich culture, philosophy, and fields such as astronomy and traditional medicine. The Indian subcontinent in ancient times was home to centers of philosophy and religion such as Nalanda and Takshashila, which attracted scholars from other parts of Asia and the Middle East. During the colonial period, the British had a very strong influence on the Indian higher education system, and the focus of Indian scholars turned to the United Kingdom and consequently to Western approaches to medicine, law, and the sciences. The education system of the U.S. had yet to emerge as an attractive alternative for pursuit of higher education.

Higher education relations between India and the U.S. could broadly be described under two categories: individual scholar visits across national borders and institutional exchanges in educational collaboration. The following section describes the nature of these educational relations and how they have evolved over the years. An examination of these may lead to new visions for the coming decade of exchange between India and the U.S.

Individual Scholar Visits

Studying Abroad

Students from India have been traveling abroad in large numbers to western universities for several decades now. Soon after Indian independence in 1947, Indian students began looking beyond traditional destinations, which include former colonial powers like the U.K. India's early association with the Soviet Union encouraged Indian students to study there, but soon the flow of students was diverted to the U.S. Indian students also sought higher education in countries such as Germany, Australia, and Canada, but the U.S. remains the destination of choice. The growth in numbers of Indian students studying in the U.S. has been phenomenal and continues to increase, thus providing a strong basis for Indo-U.S. linkages in higher education.

There was a time in India when the large exodus of Indian students to the U.S. was considered a sign of worry, as it was considered to constitute "brain drain" from the Indian soil. However, academic linkages established between the two countries were so strong that the mobility of students could not realistically be restricted. Indian nationals abroad were also repatriating funds to India in sizable quantities. Further, overseas Indians could also utilize their expertise in India through their periodic visits. With this in mind, the Indian government started looking at this growing exodus as a means of creating a "brain bank" that would enhance the Indian economy. Consequently, there have been no efforts to reduce the growing number of Indian students going to the United States. Securing visas for studying in the U.S. has always been a concern for Indian students, but even the 9/11 terrorist attack did not affect the opportunities for Indian students provided they could establish a genuine reason for studying in the United States. In the recent past, Indian students have started returning home as employment opportunities in India have increased. Several U.S. corporations have also set up their branch offices and R&D units in India, thus adding incentive for Indian students to return. This new trend is an outcome of growth in Indo-U.S. educational relations and could also be one of the areas that will strengthen the overall Indo-U.S. relationship. The visits of individual Indian students to the U.S. are perhaps the most important factor that has strengthened Indo-U.S. educational cooperation.

It is, however, unfortunate that this flow of Indian students to the U.S. has not been matched by corresponding visits of American students to India. Although the reasons for the lack of mobility of American students to India are understandable, both governments have to evolve new strategies for reducing this disparity. In view of recent positive developments in India and its new status among developing countries, the genuine interest of the American students and scholars wanting to visit India is likely to grow, but institutional mechanisms on both sides, particularly in India, have to be radically changed to attract more American students.

The Fulbright Program

The Fulbright exchange program of the U.S. government, currently operating in more than 155 countries, was envisaged by its creator, Senator J. William Fulbright, as a way to promote mutual understanding through educational exchanges between U.S. citizens and citizens of partner countries. The Fulbright Program in India had started in 1950 with the establishment of the United States Educational Foundation in India (USEFI), through a binational agreement. In July 2008, as a result of the enhanced partnership between India and the U.S. governments, the name of the foundation was changed to United States-India Educational Foundation (USIEF; see www.usief.org.in). USIEF has awarded around 16,400 Fulbright and other grants to U.S. and Indian scholars, professionals, and students since its inception in 1950. The Fulbright family in India and in the U.S. has become a wide network of individuals demonstrating academic and professional excellence. A large number of students and academics have established long-term relationships with academic institutions in both countries.

Institutional Exchanges

Immediately after Indian independence in 1947, India continued to model its universities after the British system, but Indian scholars soon started looking to other countries for new educational models. Developed countries like the U.S., the Soviet Union, and Germany encouraged collaboration initiatives with the Indian higher education system. In the decades after independence, both government and private initiatives enhanced institutional educational linkages between India and the U.S.

The IIT Kanpur Model

Soon after national independence, the Indian government, which played a primary role in supporting higher education, was keen to benefit from modern scientific and technological developments. The government wanted to develop institutions in India that would produce the scientists and engineers that would play a critical role in the modernization of independent India. In the early sixties, a unique experiment in international collaboration in higher education was initiated. India decided to collaborate with individual countries including the U.S., UK, Germany, and the Soviet Union, requesting that each country set up an Institute of Technology in different cities of India, with the support of the Indian government.

In the early sixties, the formation of the Indian Institute of Technology at Kanpur was perhaps the first major institutional initiative in Indo-U.S. collaboration in higher education. The Kanpur Indo-American Programme, involving a consortium of nine top-tier U.S. universities, helped set up research laboratories and academic programs through extensive exchanges of faculty and students. Under the guidance of economist John Kenneth Galbraith, who at that time was the U.S. Ambassador to India, IIT Kanpur became the first institute in India to offer computer science education. The earliest computer courses were started in August 1963 on an IBM 1620 system, a novelty then even in many North American and European universities.

It is this kind of collaboration in institution-building that is likely to be an enduring educational exchange activity between India and the U.S. With new governments in both countries looking at opportunities for future collaboration, the IIT Kanpur example could prove to be very useful. The Indian government today is in a better position than in the past to play a substantial role in providing academic leadership in forming joint Indo-U.S. higher educational institutions in India—and perhaps in the U.S., too.

University-Level Exchanges through MOUs

Over the years, there have been several institution-level initiatives by Indian and American universities to enhance academic collaboration. Based on the visits of individual senior scholars, universities on both sides have expressed a desire to continue exchanging faculty (and occasionally students) in order to strengthen institutional linkages. These interests are formalized through written Memoranda of Understanding (MOUs) signed between the two educational institutions. A large number of such MOUs have been signed by universities on both sides. Unfortunately, the intentions expressed in these MOUs are not always realized. After initial euphoria about the signing of the MOUs, the programs often remain more or less on paper. There are many reasons for inaction on both sides that need to be explored, but the primary reason is lack of resources and incompatible research interests on the two sides. The variations in the academic cycles of the two institutions also prove to be a hindrance to the free flow of scholars. On the surface, this mode of educational exchanges has great potential to strengthen Indo-U.S. educational relations, but a more realistic approach and more efficient program management tools have to be introduced on both sides to take full advantage of MOUs.

Indo-U.S. Institutions in Social Sciences

American Institute of Indian Studies (AIIS)

In 1961, a consortium of American universities interested in Indian studies founded the American Institute of Indian Studies (AIIS) in Chicago. With a large number of American scholars showing interest in Indian studies, the activities of AIIS expanded rapidly, and it soon opened offices in India. For more than 30 years, the institute has provided fellowship support for senior American scholars and PhD candidates. So far, 3,500 American scholars have received fellowships through AIIS. The research work of these scholars has led to the publication of hundreds of books and thousands of articles. The core of *India and America*, a highly respected volume published by the institute, is a listing of these books. Today the institute receives primary funding from the Smithsonian Institution, the U.S. State Department, the Council of American Overseas Research Centers, the National Science Foundation, the National Endowment for the Humanities, and the U.S. Department of Education. Activities in India have been consolidated in the AIIS international headquarters building, located in Gurgaon, close to Delhi's international airport. American funds have declined as a percentage of all funding, but AIIS is making all efforts to continue funding its activities through private sources.

AIIS has made a major contribution to America's understanding of Indian history and culture. These efforts should be continued and receive support in the future.

American Studies Research Center (ASRC)

To complement the efforts of AIIS, in 1964 the U.S. government set up an American Studies Research Center (ASRC) on the five-acre campus of Osmania University in Hyderabad. A large number of Indian scholars received fellowships to conduct research in American studies, primarily focusing on American literature and political science. The funding for ASRC was originally provided from the Public Law 480 rupee reserve, which was funding from the U.S. government based on American grain sale to India. It became customary for the director of this institute to be an American Fulbright scholar choosing to work in India for an extended period. Unfortunately, the PL 480 funds were no longer available for programs in India as of 1998, as per the understanding of the two governments, and the future of the ASRC was uncertain. The Fulbright program in India also suffered during this period, since it had also received substantial funds under PL 480. The Fulbright program slowly recovered from the crisis. In 2000, the ASRC converted into an institution under the name of Indo-American Institute for International Studies (IACIS) and started looking for private funding. Yet these efforts to save this Indo-U.S. collaboration did not succeed. Finally, in 2006, Osmania University took over ASRC assets and converted the institute into an autonomous body of the university, the Osmania University Centre for International Programs (OUCIP). With some grant funding from U.S. sources, American studies programs may continue at OUCIP, though in reduced form.

It is sad that these two institutions that focused on the social science aspects of the Indo-U.S. relationship could not continue to flourish as originally intended. One hopes that the recent initiatives taken by the two governments will once again give a boost to American and Indian studies, which are so important in efforts to build a long-term relationship between the two countries. Science and technology are perhaps the new flavors of our times, but we cannot ignore the role of social sciences in the development of our two societies.

Indo-U.S. Science and Technology Forum

Another initiative that India and the U.S. have taken is the Indo-U.S. Science and Technology Forum (IUSSTF), established under an agreement between the Governments of India and the U.S. in March 2000. This is an autonomous, not-for-profit society that promotes Indo-U.S. bilateral collaborations in science, technology, engineering, and biomedical research through substantive interaction among government, academia, and industry. While the IUSSTF will undoubtedly give impetus to specific international research collaborations, perhaps if these joint projects also offer scholarships or find other ways to involve students, this forum could strengthen Indo-U.S. academic relations more broadly.

Future Challenges and Opportunities

The various types of educational collaboration mentioned above will no doubt continue to strengthen Indo-U.S. educational relations in the future, but there are more ways to work toward closer ties between the two countries. This section contains some suggestions for further strengthening Indo-U.S. relations.

Student Mobility—Attracting More American Students to India

Students should continue to play a major role in any activities that are taken up under the new Indo-U.S. collaborative initiatives. Students are the future "ambassadors" for strengthening the ties between the two countries. To this extent, the existing flow of Indian students to the U.S. should be much more broad-based and should cover areas beyond science and engineering. Students should be encouraged and supported to pursue studies in fields such as journalism, communications, and humanities and liberal arts disciplines including history and philosophy. These studies could last from two to three months, with Indian students receiving academic credit toward degrees in India. More importantly, Indian universities should develop suitable semester-length "study India programs" to attract American students seeking to study abroad. Close collaboration with American universities should be ensured so that courses offered under the "study India programs" are recognized for credit in American universities. Both governments should encourage this reverse flow of American students by offering attractive scholarships and developing quality programs of study.

Institutional Exchanges Under the Fulbright Program

While the traditional Fulbright Scholar Program will retain its importance, several other Fulbright programs could potentially support institutional exchanges. Existing programs including Scholar-in-Residence, Visiting Lecturer Fellowships, and the Fulbright Teacher Exchange Program could be offered on an institutional basis in the future, as could joint research projects. Institutions could be chosen for a fixed period of three years, for example, and then the programs could be rotated to benefit other institutions as well. Such an arrangement would strengthen collaboration at the institutional level. This may be a new approach for the Fulbright program, which has traditionally focused on the individual scholar. However, the nature and prestige of the program could help build greater institutional linkages between the two countries—linkages that are very weak today. Universities entering into agreements through MOUs could be encouraged to apply for the Fulbright scholarships under the institutional umbrella.

Binational Universities Under the Indo-U.S. Joint Working Group

Considering the success of IIT Kanpur, it may be worthwhile to develop new binational universities in India under the Indo-U.S. Joint Working Group in education, set up in June 2009. Recently, the Indian government announced that it would welcome well-known U.S. universities to set up campuses in India. An appropriate bill is being proposed to the Indian parliament.

In India, there is great concern for raising the gross enrollment ratio (GER)—the percentage of students who are actually pursuing higher education compared to the total college-aged cohort—from the present figure of about 10 percent to 15 percent or more. To achieve this, one solution would be to increase the number of higher education institutions in the country. The government has already proposed the creation of a large number of new universities in the country. The question of easing regulations on the activities of foreign universities in India had been dragging on for a long time under the previous government, but major higher education reforms now being proposed in India may allow joint ventures between India and the U.S. to come into existence. If India could host campuses of top-tier U.S. universities and other high-quality U.S. institutions, this would greatly help to strengthen Indo-U.S. educational relations and at the same time address some of the key problems faced by higher education in India. U.S. universities could also use this opportunity to enhance their research activities through the participation of talented Indian students and faculty. The industrial research and development units set up by many multinational companies on Indian soil could also benefit from the local skilled work force that such institutions would help to create.

If such binational universities prove to be a success—as IIT Kanpur has been—perhaps they could host more international students who want to study in India and gain the benefits of U.S. higher education without having to travel to the U.S., allowing them to save on educational costs.

Indo-U.S. Science and Technology Forum

The Indo-U.S. Science and Technology Forum (IUSSTF) could complement its research projects by pursuing an educational agenda as well. Research scholarships could be made available to Indian and U.S. students for work on IUSSTF joint projects, which would count toward credit for graduate study at home while also offering an opportunity to work with foreign scholars and possibly to travel abroad. As far as Indian students are concerned, doing research under such a program would greatly expand their career opportunities. The American students could also see this as an opportunity to understand how global research is conducted in a developing country like India.

Providing Educational Services Globally—Promoting International Education

Education has lately been considered part of the "service sector" under the General Agreement on Trade in Services (GATS), placing developments in education squarely within larger trends of economic globalization. India and the U.S. are signatories to GATS and have a common interest in providing education services. The U.S. currently holds an advantage in providing such services globally, but India could export educational services to other countries in Asia and the Middle East at competitive rates (as has already been demonstrated by Indian branch campuses that currently exist in these regions). Perhaps a joint Indo-U.S. effort to promote educational services to third countries could boost academic and economic activity in both countries.

During the past few years, India has increasingly focused attention on the impact of globalization on higher education in India. The government is still reluctant to open its doors to foreign institutions, but recent changes in government policy may lead to additional opportunities for international educators in India.

In order to promote international education in India, private universities and the corporate sector have organized conferences on various aspects of the field. The Federation of Indian Chambers of Commerce and Industry (FICCI), under the auspices of its Education Committee, has organized annual education summits with participation from government representatives, private and public education institutions, and foreign university representatives. The Manipal Group, in cooperation with other private universities, has set up a forum that organizes annual conferences under the banner of "Emerging Directions in Global Education" (EDGE). These conferences have resulted in numerous recommendations for the internationalization of Indian higher education. FICCI and EDGE should also be used to strengthen Indo-U.S. education relations in the future.

Conclusion

The demand for higher education in India and in the U.S. continues to grow. With globalization continuing to affect the education sector, opportunities for economic growth through promotion of higher education are increasing. India and the U.S. have a common interest in collaborating in a number of areas; exchanges in higher education between India and the U.S. should be a priority and will greatly help in strengthening relations between the two countries. The newly established Indo-U.S. Joint Working Group in education, the private education sector, and the corporate sector will also develop new forums for promoting international education in India. Based on an examination of educational relations over the last four decades, several new initiatives by individual scholars and at the institutional level have been proposed for the consideration of the higher education community and the governments of the two countries.

REFERENCES

Indo-Asian News Service. (2009, June 18). We need 'US-India 3.0' in ties: Hillary Clinton (Lead). Retrieved from http://www.thaindian.com/newsportal/sci-tech/we-need-us-india-30-in-ties-hillary-clinton-lead_100206443.html

About the Contributors

Pawan Agarwal is an Indian civil servant and has served in the Ministry of Human Resource Development and the apex body for higher education, where he developed substantial expertise in higher education policy and practice. From 2005 to 2006, he was a Fulbright New Century Scholar. His recent book, *Indian Higher Education: Envisioning the Future*, is the most comprehensive and up-to-date review of Indian higher education so far and has received a positive response in India and abroad. His other important studies and publications are on private higher education, higher education and labor markets, comparative study from a Latin American perspective, privatization and internationalization trends in South Asian countries, status and prospects of liberal arts education, and global student mobility.

Philip G. Altbach is J. Donald Monan, S.J., University Professor and director of the Center for International Higher Education in the Lynch School of Education at Boston College. He was the 2004–2006 Distinguished Scholar Leader for the New Century Scholars initiative of the Fulbright program. He has been a senior associate of the Carnegie Foundation for the Advancement of Teaching. He is author of *Turmoil and Transition: The International Imperative in Higher Education*, *Comparative Higher Education*, *Student Politics in America*, and other books. He coedited the *International Handbook of Higher Education*. His most recent book is *World Class Worldwide: Transforming Research Universities in Asia and Latin America*. He is chairperson of the International Advisory Council of the Graduate School of Education at Shanghai Jiao Tong University.

Rajika Bhandari is director of research and evaluation at the Institute of International Education (IIE) in New York where she leads two major research projects—*Open Doors* and *Project Atlas*—that measure international higher education mobility at the domestic (U.S.) and international level. She is a frequent speaker and author on the topic of mobility, serves on the Global Advisory Council of the Observatory on Borderless Higher Education, and is also on the editorial board of the *Journal of Studies in International Education*. Before joining IIE, Bhandari was a senior researcher at MPR Associates, an educational research firm in Berkeley, California, that provides research and evaluation services to the U.S. Department of Education. She also served as the assistant director for evaluation at the Mathematics and Science Education Network at the University of North Carolina at Chapel Hill. She holds a doctoral degree in psychology from North Carolina State University and a BA (Honors) in Psychology from the University of Delhi, India.

Sudhanshu Bhushan is professor and head, Department of Higher and Professional Education at National University of Educational Planning and Administration, New Delhi. He conducts research in the area of higher education policy and planning and specializes in the field of internationalization of higher education. He is currently researching topics including foreign education providers in India, the financing of the higher education component of India's Eleventh Five Year Plan, and self-financing courses in colleges. His book on restructuring higher education in India was released in October 2009 by Rawat Publications in Jaipur, India, and Bookwell India is expected to publish his book on public financing and deregulated fees in higher education in November 2009. Bhushan provides academic support to the federal government and central bodies including the Planning Commission of India and the University Grants Commission. He conducts capacity-building programs for senior higher education administrators and leads workshops and seminars in higher education policy and planning.

Rahul Choudaha is associate director of development and innovation at World Education Services, New York. He has expertise in international higher education with emphasis on strategic management, market development, student mobility, policy, and collaborations. Previously, he led international recruitment and marketing at the Indian School of Business, Hyderabad. He is currently serving on the committee of the National Association of Graduate Admissions Professionals (NAGAP) and the Association of International Education Administrators (AIEA). Choudaha has published papers and presented at the conferences of several professional organizations and institutions, including AIEA, NAFSA, ASHE, AACRAO, NAGAP, NASPA, QS-APPLE, IIM-Bangalore, IIT-Mumbai, and Harvard Graduate School of Education. He received the NAGAP Research Grant in 2008 and the Outstanding Doctoral Student Award at the University of Denver. Choudaha also writes a blog on education at www.DrEducation.com. He earned his PhD in higher education from the University of Denver and holds an MBA in marketing and an undergraduate degree in engineering.

Darla K. Deardorff is executive director of the Association of International Education Administrators (AIEA), based at Duke University. Editor of the recently published *Sage Handbook of Intercultural Competence*, she has published widely on international education. With over 15 years of experience in the field, she teaches courses in international education and intercultural communication and is on the faculty of the Summer Institute of Intercultural Communication in Portland, Oregon. She has given invited talks and workshops around the world on intercultural competence and assessment and serves as a consultant and trainer on these topics. Deardorff has received several awards related to her work, and the intercultural competence models developed from her research are used in numerous countries. She received her master's and doctoral degrees from North Carolina State University.

Prabhakar Lavakare began his career at the Tata Institute of Fundamental Research, Mumbai. After two decades of research, he joined the Ministry of Science and Technology (India) as an advisor and served as the secretary of the Science Advisory Council to the Prime Minister from 1986 to 1990. Lavakare has been a consultant to UNESCO and UNDP. On his retirement from government service, he served as executive director of the U.S. Educational Foundation in India until 1999. He is a member of the Board of Management of the Symbiosis International University in Pune, India. He has published over 50 papers, edited four books, and authored two popular science books. He is a founding member of the Education Committee of the Federation of Indian Chambers of Commerce and Industry (FICCI). In 1959, he attended the University of Rochester as a Fulbright scholar and received his PhD in physics in 1963.

Ranjini Manian is founder and CEO of Global Adjustments Services Pvt. Ltd., India's premier relocation and cross-cultural services company. She is a multicultural expert with one foot planted firmly in India's traditions and the other roaming the world seeking to understand differences. Manian is the editor of India's only cultural magazine for expatriates, *At a Glance –Understanding India*, a Global Adjustments publication. She is also the architect of www.globalindian.com, a cross-cultural e-learning portal in India. The Global Adjustments India Immersion Center in Chennai, which facilitates the meeting of cultures, is her brainchild. Author of *Doing Business in India for Dummies*, Manian also writes columns in leading Indian business dailies and is the only Indian on the Women's Leadership Board at Harvard University. She holds a bachelor's degree from Elphinstone College, Mumbai, and a diploma in French literature from the Sorbonne, University of Paris. Besides English, Manian is fluent in several Indian and foreign languages, including French and Japanese.

Ajit Motwani is director of IIE's offices in India, responsible for implementing projects in India with the goal of strengthening U.S.-India academic and professional exchanges. He has over 28 years of experience in diverse fields. Prior to joining IIE, he was executive director of Educational Consultants India Limited (Ed.CIL) under the Ministry of Human Resource Development, promoting new ventures to expand education in India from the primary through the tertiary level. Ed.CIL is also the central agency charged with promoting Indian education abroad. He has worked to expand cooperation between India and the Association of Southeast Asian Nations (ASEAN) in the area of human resource development, visited Finland for guest lectures to international business students, and spoken at national and international conferences and seminars. Motwani has an MBA degree from the Faculty of Management Studies, Delhi University, and a B.Tech. from the Indian Institute of Technology, Kanpur.

Shobha Naidu has served as senior manager, cross-cultural services, at Global Adjustments Bangalore since 2006. She develops training content and conducts cross-cultural training for Indian and expatriate professionals engaged in the IT and Information Technology Enabled Services (ITES) sectors. Previously, she worked with Aide et Action, a French international NGO, in the field of elementary education and corporate social responsibility. In this capacity, she was a cultural interpreter in France and India, working with university students, corporations, and foundations.

Naidu is an active member of SIETAR India (Society for Intercultural Education, Training and Research) and presented a paper at their 2008 global conference in Granada. She coauthored a chapter for the *Sage Handbook of Intercultural Competence*, edited by Darla Deardorff. She received an MPhil in development studies from the Graduate Institute of Development Studies, Geneva, and is fluent in French.

Sam Pitroda is an internationally respected development thinker, telecom inventor, and entrepreneur who has spent 44 years in information and communications technology and related human and national developments. Credited with having laid the foundation for and ushered in India's technology and telecommunications revolution in the 1980s, Pitroda has been a leading campaigner to help bridge the global digital divide. During his tenure as advisor to Prime Minister Rajiv Gandhi in the 1980s, Pitroda headed six technology missions related to telecommunications, water, literacy, immunization, dairy, and oil seeds. He was also the founder and first chairman of India's Telecom Commission. Pitroda was chairman of India's National Knowledge Commission (2005–2009), an advisory body to the Prime Minister of India set up to provide a blueprint for reform of the knowledge-related institutions and infrastructure in the country. He is currently advisor to the Prime Minister of India on public information infrastructure and innovations. He holds close to 100 worldwide patents and has published and lectured widely in the U.S., Europe, Latin America, and Asia.

Nicole Ranganath is director, international and outreach initiatives at the University of California, Davis. As director, she partners with faculty, funding agencies, and overseas universities to initiate new international and outreach programs at UC Davis. Her area of expertise is launching new academic programs with higher education institutions in Asia, especially India, and in developing new faculty resources to stimulate multidisciplinary international research collaborations. She is also the UC Davis campus representative for the Fulbright scholar programs. She earned her PhD in history from the University of Illinois, Urbana-Champaign, focusing on the South Asian diaspora, and earned a BA in anthropology from the University of California, Berkeley.

Alina L. Romanowski was appointed in May 2009 as Deputy Assistant Secretary for Academic Programs in the Department of State's (DOS) Bureau of Educational and Cultural Affairs (ECA) where she oversees all academic programs, including the Fulbright Program, the Humphrey Program, Gilman Scholarships and English Language Programs. Previously, she served for almost four years as ECA's Deputy Assistant Secretary for Professional and Cultural Exchanges. Romanowski came to DOS in 2003 to establish an office for the President's Middle East Partnership Initiative, serving as its first director. She also served as Acting Deputy Assistant Secretary in the Bureau of Near Eastern Affairs. Romanowski served at the Defense Department (DOD) for almost 14 years in various senior positions involving Near East and South Asia, including Deputy Assistant Secretary of Defense for that region. She came to DOD from the Central Intelligence Agency in 1990 after serving 10 years as an intelligence analyst on the Near East and South Asia region.

Krishna Vedula is professor of chemical engineering and dean emeritus, University of Massachusetts Lowell. As dean of engineering, he was recognized for his leadership in building unique partnerships with businesses, elementary and secondary schools, state agencies, and other educational institutions. Vedula is currently the cofounder and executive director of the Indo-US Collaboration in Engineering Education (IUCEE), which aims to improve the quality and global relevance of engineering education in India and the U.S. Vedula also assists the provost of UMass Lowell in building international partnerships all over the world. Vedula has a B.Tech. from IIT, India; an MS from Drexel University; and a PhD from Michigan Tech University, all in materials engineering. He has 25 years of academic teaching and research experience in materials science and engineering.

Vivek Wadhwa is a senior research associate with the Labor and Worklife Program at Harvard Law School and an executive in residence/adjunct professor at the Pratt School of Engineering at Duke University. He helps students prepare for the real world, lectures in class, and leads groundbreaking research projects. He is also an advisor to several start-up companies, a columnist for BusinessWeek.com, and a contributor to several international publications. Since joining Duke University in August 2005, he has researched globalization, its impact on the engineering profession, and the sources of the U.S. competitive advantage. His work has been cited in over 1,000 national and international media outlets over a 30-month period. Before joining Duke University, Wadhwa was a technology executive in the field of investment banking and founded Relativity Technologies. He is founding president of the Carolinas chapter of The IndUS Entrepreneurs (TIE), a nonprofit global network intended to foster entrepreneurship. Wadhwa holds an MBA from New York University and a BA in computing studies from the Canberra University in Australia.

U.S.-India International Academic Partnership Activities

The following contains information about currently active partnerships between U.S. and Indian universities. Each partnership is documented on at least one of the participating institutions' websites. The list was compiled by IIE, drawing upon the existing resources maintained by USIEF and other organizations, and integrating several existing lists of programs and agreements maintained by IIE. Sources include:

- "Off-shore activities of US Universities in India," an unpublished list compiled and maintained by the United States-India Educational Foundation (USIEF);

- The Association of Indian Universities (AIU) publication *Directory of Foreign Providers of Higher Education in India, 2006*;

- The USAID-HED publication *Lessons Learned from Reviews of Higher Education Partnerships in South Asia*;

- The 2009–2010 editions of *IIEPassport: Academic Year Abroad* and *IIEPassport: Short-Term Study Abroad*, which list study-abroad opportunities for U.S. students by country;

- A review of recent articles covering the U.S.-India educational relationship, including pieces in the *Chronicle of Higher Education, Inside Higher Ed*, and *Time*; and

- Independent online research.

This is not a comprehensive list of all partnerships and does not include activities planned for the future, dormant MOUs, individual faculty projects, or partnerships not currently promoted outside the participating institutions. All web links are active as of August 27, 2009.

U.S.-India International Academic Partnership Activities
Alphabetical by U.S. institution

Auburn University Undergraduate Engineering Program - India
U.S. Institution: Auburn University
Indian Institution: Maharaja Agrasen Institute of Technology, Delhi
Web reference: http://www.eng.auburn.edu/programs/gei/india/

Ball State University student exchange program
U.S. Institution: Ball State University
Indian Institution: Annamalai University, Tamil Nadu
Web reference: http://cms.bsu.edu/Academics/CentersandInstitutes/Rinker/
                       StudyAbroad/ExplorePlacestoGo/ListofAllProgramsandLocations.aspx

Student exchange program for MBA students

U.S. Institution: Baruch College CUNY, Zicklin Business School

Indian Institution: Indian Institute of Management, Kolkata

Web reference: https://zicklin.baruch.cuny.edu/centers/weissman/study-abroad/where/rprograms/india.htm

---

Broward College India study programs

U.S. Institution: Broward College

Indian Institution: International Center for Management and Indian Studies

Web reference: http://www.broward.edu/Sandbox/print/page17858.html

---

Brown University student exchanges

U.S. Institution: Brown University

Indian Institution: St. Stephen's College or Lady Shri Ram College for Women

Web reference: http://www.brown.edu/Administration/OIP/programs/india/

Carnegie Mellon's Master of Science in Information Technology (MSIT) degree program with specializations in Software Engineering and Embedded Software Engineering

U.S. Institution: Carnegie Mellon University

Indian Institution: SSN School of Advanced Software Engineering

Web reference: http://sase.ssn.edu.in/

Champlain College software engineering, hospitality management, and business programs

U.S. Institution: Champlain College

Indian Institution: The International College at St. Xavier's Technical Institute, Mumbai

Web reference: http://www.champlain.edu/Study-Abroad/Mumbai-Campus.html

---

Clemson University student exchange program

U.S. Institution: Clemson University

Indian Institution: Ansal Institute of Technology (AIT)

Web reference: http://www.aitgurgaon.org/AboutUs/AcademicLinkages1.html
http://www.clemson.edu/ia/abroad/exchange.html

MPS (Master of Professional Studies) in Food Science / M.Tech (Master of Technology) in Food Processing and Marketing and MPS in Plant Breeding / M.Tech in Biotechnology and Business Management

U.S. Institution: Cornell University

Indian Institution: Tamil Nadu Agricultural University

Web reference: http://taupg.tnau.ac.in/

Off-campus programs in Asian and Middle Eastern studies/women's and gender studies

U.S. Institution: Dartmouth College
Indian Institution: University of Hyderabad's Study in India Program (SIP)
Web reference: http://ocp-prod.dartmouth.edu/ocp/prod/index.cfm?FuseAction=Programs.View
Program&Program_ID=0E0773724F777102710170020E1F770608001B0C7309
006B70770606730201717306057Б7A030100&Type=O&sType=O

Davidson College Fall Semester in India Program

U.S. Institution: Davidson College
Indian Institution: Madras Christian College
Web reference: http://www3.davidson.edu/cms/x17266.xml

Duke University joint MBA programs

U.S. Institution: Duke University, Fuqua School of Business
Indian Institution: India Institute of Management, Bangalore, and the Indian School of Business, Hyderabad
Web reference: http://www.fuqua.duke.edu/about/locations/india/

The Global Diabetes Research Center

U.S. Institution: Emory University
Indian Institution: The Madras Diabetes Research Foundation
Web reference: http://globaldiabetes.org/about.html

Dual Degree Program (DDP) in management

U.S. Institution: Fairleigh Dickinson University, Silberman College of Business
Indian Institution: Alliance Business School, Bangalore
Web reference: http://view.fdu.edu/default.aspx?id=551

Harvard University scholarly exchanges

U.S. Institution: Harvard University
Indian Institution: National Centre for Biological Sciences (NCBS), Jawaharlal Nehru Centre for Advanced Scientific Research, and Indian Institute of Science
Web reference: http://www.summer.harvard.edu/2009/programs/abroad/bangalore/default.jsp

ISU Exchange program agreement for engineering students

U.S. Institution: Idaho State University
Indian Institution: S.R. Engineering College (SREC)
Web reference: http://www2.isu.edu/headlines/?p=880

Two-way graduate and undergraduate exchange programs focusing on criminal justice and Indian studies

U.S. Institution: Illinois State University
Indian Institution: University of Madras
Web reference: http://www.internationalstudies.ilstu.edu/international_linkages/

Democracy and Governance in India - Summer Program

U.S. Institution: Indiana University - Bloomington

Indian Institution: National Law School of India

Web reference: http://www.indiana.edu/~overseas/flyers/bangalore.html

Research collaboration in areas of natural resource management and food sciences

U.S. Institution: Kansas State University

Indian Institution: Punjab Agricultural University

Web reference: http://www.pau.edu/index.php?_act=manageLink&DO=
firstLink&intSubID=75

Joint Master of Science in Automotive Engineering

U.S. Institution: Lawrence Technological University

Indian Institution: International Institute of Information Technology, Pune

Web reference: http://www.ltu.edu/provosts_office/international.asp#India

Study Abroad for Veterinary Students in India

U.S. Institution: Michigan State University

Indian Institution: Madras Veterinary College in Chennai

Web reference: http://studyabroad.msu.edu/programs/indiavet.html

Study abroad in electrical engineering and computer science

U.S. Institution: Milwaukee School of Engineering

Indian Institution: Manipal Academy of Higher Education - International Center for Applied Sciences (ICAS)

Web reference: http://www.msoe.edu/academics/study_abroad/manipal.shtml

Missouri School of Journalism faculty exchange and student exchange programs

U.S. Institution: Missouri School of Journalism

Indian Institution: International School of Media and Entertainment Studies (ISOMES)

Web reference: http://www.isomes.com/ViewDetailHome.aspx?id=14

Missouri State University exchange program

U.S. Institution: Missouri State University

Indian Institution: Lal Bahadur Shastri Institute of Management

Web reference: http://international.missouristate.edu/ibp/62451.htm

NDSU-AIT twinning agreement

U.S. Institution: North Dakota State University

Indian Institution: Ansal Institute of Technology (AIT)

Web reference: http://www.ndsu.edu/international/study_abroad_main/programs/
sponsored_programs/india/

Oakland University faculty exchange program

U.S. Institution: Oakland University (Michigan), School of Business Administration
Indian Institution: Symbiosis Institute of International Business
Web reference: http://www.siib.ac.in/contents.aspx?id=49&lid=17&pid=15

Exchanges of experts, research and equipment in agriculture, veterinary and animal science, agricultural engineering, home science, and allied science

U.S. Institution: Ohio State University
Indian Institution: Punjab Agricultural University
Web reference: http://www.pau.edu/index.php?_act=manageLink&DO=firstLink&intSubID=75

OHIO-India MBA program

U.S. Institution: Ohio University, College of Business
Indian Institution: Christ Education Society
Web reference: http://www.ohiochrist.edu/content.php?p_id=1

KPIT-Cummins Internship

U.S. Institution: Purdue University
Indian Institution: KPIT-Cummins
Web reference: http://www.purdue.edu/discoverypark/international/studentOpportunities.php

Twinning program in engineering fields

U.S. Institution: The RUSS College of Engineering and Technology at Ohio University
Indian Institution: Manipal Academy of Higher Education- International Center for Applied Sciences (ICAS)
Web reference: http://www.manipal.edu/manipalsite/users/ICASLandingPage.aspx?se=Deccan-Herald&kw=display&cat=#

Rutgers University study abroad

U.S. Institution: Rutgers University
Indian Institution: St. Stephen's College
Web reference: http://studyabroad.rutgers.edu/program_india.html

Salisbury University intersession study in India

U.S. Institution: Salisbury University
Indian Institution: University of Pune
Web reference: http://www.salisbury.edu/intled/studyabroad/winter/india/

Scholarly exchanges, collaborative research, and joint publications

U.S. Institution: San Jose State University
Indian Institution: Punjab Agricultural University
Web reference: http://www.pau.edu/index.php?_act=manageLink&DO=firstLink&intSubID=75

Women's leadership programs

U.S. Institution: Simmons College, School of Management
Indian Institution: Indian School of Business at Hyderabad, Indian Institute of Management - Calcutta, and private sector partners
Web reference: http://www.simmons.edu/som/mba/international/

Slippery Rock University semester and year-long study abroad

U.S. Institution: Slippery Rock University
Indian Institution: University of Rajasthan
Web reference: http://www.sru.edu/pages/10736.asp

ITM-SNHU Partnership

U.S. Institution: Southern New Hampshire University
Indian Institution: Institute for Technology and Management (ITM)
Web reference: http://www.snhu.edu/2880.asp

Stanford Graduate School of Business (GSB) and the Indian Institute of Management (Bangalore) Link (SAIL) program

U.S. Institution: Stanford Graduate School of Business (GSB)
Indian Institution: Indian Institute of Management - Bangalore
Web reference: http://www.gsb.stanford.edu/gmp/programs/sail.html

Master of Science in Management of Information Technology Enabled Services (MITES) program

U.S. Institution: State University of New York at Buffalo, School of Management
Indian Institution: Amrita University
Web reference: http://mgt.buffalo.edu/programs/abroad/MITES http://amritauniversity.info/index.html

International Bachelor's Degree Program

U.S. Institution: Temple University, The Fox School of Business and Management
Indian Institution: L.N. Welingkar Institute of Management Development and Research, Mumbai
Web reference: http://sbm.temple.edu/igms/undergrad.html

International MBA Program

U.S. Institution: Temple University, The Fox School of Business and Management
Indian Institution: L.N. Welingkar Institute of Management Development and Research, Mumbai
Web reference: http://www.welingkar.org/Welingkar/v1/Programmes/InterPrgIMBA.asp?br=2&section=Programs http://sbm.temple.edu/imba/

Post-Graduate Diploma in International Finance (PGDIF)

U.S. Institution: Tulane University
Indian Institution: Globsyn Business School
Web reference: http://www.gbs.edu.in/tulane/Agreement.pdf

University of Arkansas Global India study abroad program
U.S. Institution: University of Arkansas
Indian Institution: International Center for Management and India Studies (ICMIS)
Web reference: http://india.uark.edu

Joint projects in biotechnology and biofuel
U.S. Institution: University of California, Berkeley
Indian Institution: Indian Institute of Technology (IIT), Kharagpur, West Bengal
Web reference: http://ls.berkeley.edu/?q=about-college/research-I-s/iit-kharagpur

STEP: The International Student Exchange Program of IIM Calcutta
U.S. Institution: University of California, Los Angeles, Andersen Management School
Indian Institution: Indian Institute of Management, Kolkata, West Bengal
Web reference: http://www.iimcal.ac.in/programs/step/partners.html

University of Connecticut, School of Business advanced management study abroad program
U.S. Institution: University of Connecticut, School of Business
Indian Institution: Management Development Institute (MDI), Gurgaon
Web reference: http://www.mdi.ac.in/images/pdf/Finance%20for%20Non-Finance%20Executives.pdf

Visiting student partnership
U.S. Institution: University of Dayton
Indian Institution: Sri Ramasamy Memorial University, Chennai, and Loyola Institute of
                          Business Administration
Web reference: http://liba.edu/index.php http://international.udayton.edu/resources/partners.htm

Cooperative academic interchange
U.S. Institution: University of Florida
Indian Institution: Punjab Agricultural University
Web reference: http://www.pau.edu/index.php?_act=manageLink&DO=firstLink&intSubID=75

SAO-Law exchange
U.S. Institution: University of Illinois at Urbana-Champaign
Indian Institution: National Academy of Legal Studies and Research (NALSAR) University, Hyderabad
Web reference: https://www.studyabroad.uiuc.edu/index.cfm?FuseAction=
                          Programs.ViewProgram&Program_ID=06067671704F0700700576757606
                          1C707E7A0014010109726E0103737477010B7673077D0470047475&Type=O&sType=O

Child and Adolescent Development: Cultural Perspectives - A Punjabi Immersion Experience
U.S. Institution: University of Maryland - College Park
Indian Institution: Khalsa College of Education, Amritsar
Web reference: http://www.international.umd.edu/studyabroad/6131

East Meets West: Contrasting Public Health Priorities, Pragmatics, and Polemics in the U.S. and India

U.S. Institution: University of Maryland - College Park

Indian Institution: Manipal University

Web reference: http://www.international.umd.edu/studyabroad/8090

UNO-IIT Kharagpur academic and cultural exchange

U.S. Institution: University of Nebraska - Omaha

Indian Institution: Indian Institute of Technology, Kharagpur

Web reference: http://world.unomaha.edu/index.php?page=studyabroad&subpage=findaprogram&content=uno'sinternationallinkages

Graduate business administration courses

U.S. Institution: University of North Texas

Indian Institution: Areez Khambatta Benevolent Trust, Ahmedabad

Web reference: http://international.unt.edu/index.php?view=article&id=395&option=com_content&Itemid=183

Penn Abroad

U.S. Institution: University of Pennsylvania

Indian Institution: Lady Shri Ram College for Women

Web reference: http://sa.oip.upenn.edu/index.cfm?FuseAction=Programs.Home

Business schools collaboration

U.S. Institution: University of Pennsylvania, Wharton School of Business

Indian Institution: Indian School of Business (ISB)

Web reference: http://www.wharton.upenn.edu/academics/international/

Collaboration with the Master's of Public Health Degree

U.S. Institution: University of South Florida, The College of Public Health

Indian Institution: International Institute of Information Technology, Hyderabad

Web reference: http://health.usf.edu/publichealth/cophinternational/usflinks.html

Joint educational and research programs, including faculty exchanges

U.S. Institution: University of Southern California, Viterbi School of Engineering

Indian Institution: Indian Institute of Science, Bangalore

Web reference: http://viterbi.usc.edu/academics/globalization/iisc-bangalore.htm

USC-IIT Kharagpur research partnerships and exchanges

U.S. Institution: University of Southern California, Viterbi School of Engineering

Indian Institution: Indian Institute of Technology in Kharagpur

Web reference: http://viterbi.usc.edu/academics/globalization/research-collaborations/iit.htm

MBA exchange program
U.S. Institution: University of Texas - Austin
Indian Institution: Indian Institute of Management, Ahmedabad
Web reference: http://utdirect.utexas.edu/student/abroad/programs_detail.WBX?s_pgm_code=160026

Joint MBA program
U.S. Institution: University of Toledo
Indian Institution: PSG Institute of Management, Coimbatore
Web reference: http://www.utoledo.edu/business/InternationalStudents/IndiaPSG.html

Members of Universitas 21, an international network of 21 leading research-intensive universities in 13 countries
U.S. Institution: University of Virginia
Indian Institution: Delhi University
Web reference: http://www.universitas21.com/Member/memberdelhi.html

University of Wisconsin - Madison Study Abroad in India
U.S. Institution: University of Wisconsin - Madison
Indian Institution: Banaras Hindu University
Web reference: https://www.studyabroad.wisc.edu/programs/program.asp?program_id=84

Joint bachelor's degree programs in electronic engineering technology – avionics, airline management, and airport management
U.S. Institution: Vaughn College of Aeronautics and Technology
Indian Institution: Sreenidhi Institute of Science and Technology, Rangareddy
Web reference: http://www.vaughn.edu/admissions_sreenidhi.php

Institutional partnership for research collaboration and study abroad
U.S. Institution: Virginia Commonwealth University
Indian Institution: Postgraduate Institute of Medical Education and Research, Chandigarh
Web reference: http://www.international.vcu.edu/partnerships/universities/pgimer.html

Institutional partnership for research collaboration and study abroad
U.S. Institution: Virginia Commonwealth University
Indian Institution: Indian Institute of Technology, Kharagpur
Web reference: http://www.international.vcu.edu/partnerships/universities/iitkgp.html

Dual Degree Program: Post Graduate Diploma in Systems Management and Master's in Information Technology
U.S. Institution: Virginia Polytechnic Institute and State University
Indian Institution: S.P. Jain Institute of Management and Research, Mumbai
Web reference: http://www.international.pamplin.vt.edu/mitIndia/ http://www.spjimr.org/ pgdsm_mit/pgdsm_mit_home.asp

Graduate exchange program

U.S. Institution: Wake Forest University, Babcock Management School
Indian Institution: Indian Institute of Management, Kolkata
Web reference: http://business.wfu.edu/default.aspx?id=235

Partnership for the advancement of research, teaching, and increased cultural understanding

U.S. Institution: Washington University in St. Louis, Olin Business School
Indian Institution: Indian Institute of Management, Kolkata
Web reference: http://magazine.wustl.edu/Winter08/Frontrunners.html

MBA twinning program, undergraduate engineering transnational education program, and additional programs in the social sciences

U.S. Institution: Western Michigan University
Indian Institution: Rajagiri College
Web reference: http://international.wmich.edu/content/view/1571/2/

Undergraduate twinning program (2+2)

U.S. Institution: Western Michigan University
Indian Institution: Christ College, Bangalore
Web reference: http://www.christuniversity.in/display_article.php?fid=23&arid=14

The Fox International Fellowship Program

U.S. Institution: Yale University
Indian Institution: Jawharlal Nehru University
Web reference: http://www.yale.edu/macmillan/fif/india.html

Yale Parliamentary Leadership Program

U.S. Institution: Yale University
Indian Institution: Federation of Indian Chambers of Commerce and Industry
Web reference: http://opa.yale.edu/news/article.aspx?id=6762

IIE Information and Resources

OPEN DOORS REPORT ON INTERNATIONAL EDUCATIONAL EXCHANGE

The *Open Doors Report on International Educational Exchange*, supported by the U.S. Department of State, Bureau of Educational and Cultural Affairs, provides an annual, comprehensive statistical analysis of academic mobility between the United States and other nations, as well as trend data over 60 years.

WEBSITE: www.opendoors.iienetwork.org

THE CENTER FOR INTERNATIONAL PARTNERSHIPS IN HIGHER EDUCATION

The IIE Center for International Partnerships in Higher Education assists colleges and universities in developing and sustaining institutional partnerships with their counterparts around the world. A major initiative of the Center is the International Academic Partnerships Program, funded by the U.S. Department of Education's Fund for the Improvement of Postsecondary Education (FIPSE).

EMAIL: iapp@iie.org

ATLAS OF STUDENT MOBILITY

Project Atlas tracks migration trends of the millions of students who pursue education outside of their home countries each year. Data are collected on global student mobility patterns, country of origin, as well as leading host destinations for higher education.

WEBSITE: http://atlas.iienetwork.org

IIE STUDY ABROAD WHITE PAPER SERIES: MEETING AMERICA'S GLOBAL EDUCATION CHALLENGE

An IIE policy research initiative that addresses the issue of increasing capacity in the U.S. and abroad in order to help pave the way for substantial growth in study abroad.

• Expanding Study Abroad Capacity at U.S. Colleges and Universities (May 2009)

• Promoting Study Abroad in Science and Technology Fields (March 2009)

• Expanding U.S. Study Abroad in the Arab World: Challenges & Opportunities (February 2009)

• Expanding Education Abroad at Community Colleges (September 2008)

• Exploring Host Country Capacity for Increasing U.S. Study Abroad (May 2008)

• Current Trends in U.S. Study Abroad & the Impact of Strategic Diversity Initiatives (May 2007)

WEBSITE: www.iie.org/StudyAbroadCapacity

IIE/AIFS FOUNDATION GLOBAL EDUCATION RESEARCH REPORTS

This series explores the most pressing and under-researched issues affecting international education policy today.

- International India: A Turning Point in Educational Exchange with the U.S. (January February 2010)
- Higher Education on the Move: New Developments in Global Mobility (April 2009)
- U.S.-China Educational Exchange: Perspectives on a Growing Partnership (October 2008)

IIE PERCEPTION STUDIES

- Attitudes and Perceptions of Prospective International Students from Vietnam (February 2010)
- Attitudes and Perceptions of Prospective International Students from India (February 2010)

IIE BRIEFING PAPERS

IIE Briefing Papers are a rapid response to the changing landscape of international education, offering timely snapshots of critical issues in the field.

- The Value of International Education to U.S. Business and Industry Leaders: Key Findings from a Survey of CEOs (October 2009)
- The Three-year Bologna-compliant Degree: Responses from U.S. Graduate Schools (April 2009)
- Educational Exchange between the United States and China (July 2008)

WEBSITE: www.iie.org/researchpublications

Web Resources

OPEN DOORS ONLINE

Open Doors statistics and data tables, regional fact sheets, press information, and archives available online.

WEBSITE: http://opendoors.iienetwork.org

IIENETWORK.ORG

IIE's membership website contains articles and reports, information on best practices in the field, and many more resources for international educators.

WEBSITE: www.iienetwork.org

IIEPASSPORT.ORG

This free online search engine lists over 9,000 study abroad programs worldwide and provides advisers with hands-on tools to counsel students and promote study abroad.

WEBSITE: www.iiepassport.org

STUDY ABROAD FUNDING

This valuable funding resource helps U.S. students find funding for their study abroad.

WEBSITE: www.studyabroadfunding.org

FUNDING FOR UNITED STATES STUDY

This directory offers the most relevant data on hundreds of fellowships, grants, paid internships, and scholarships for study in the U.S.

WEBSITE: www.fundingusstudy.org

INTENSIVE ENGLISH USA

Comprehensive reference with over 500 accredited English language programs in the U.S.

WEBSITE: www.intensiveenglishusa.org

IIE RESOURCES FOR STUDY ABROAD

IIE offers a single point of entry to access valuable study abroad information, including policy research, data on study abroad trends, news coverage of new developments, fact sheets for students, and dates and deadlines for major scholarship and fellowship programs.

WEBSITE: www.iie.org/studyabroad

IIE/AIFS Foundation Global Education Research Reports

INTERNATIONAL INDIA: A TURNING POINT IN EDUCATIONAL EXCHANGE WITH THE U.S.

145

INTERNATIONALIZING THE CAMPUS

IIE administers a wealth of programs and provides a variety of services and resources to help U.S. colleges and universities develop and implement their strategies for greater campus internationalization.

WEBSITE: www.iie.org/internationalizing

FULBRIGHT PROGRAMS FOR U.S. STUDENTS

The Fulbright U.S. Student Program equips future American leaders with the skills they need to thrive in an increasingly global environment by providing funding for one academic year of study or research abroad, to be conducted after graduation from an accredited university.

SPONSOR: U.S. Department of State, Bureau of Educational and Cultural Affairs

WEBSITE: http://us.fulbrightonline.org

FULBRIGHT PROGRAMS FOR U.S. SCHOLARS

The traditional Fulbright Scholar Program sends 800 U.S. faculty and professionals abroad each year. Grantees lecture and conduct research in a wide variety of academic and professional fields.

SPONSOR: U.S. Department of State, Bureau of Educational and Cultural Affairs

WEBSITE: www.cies.org